THE SOCIO-SPIRITUAL RECIPES FOR LIVING AN EXCELLENT LIFE

*Eleven Dynamic Keys
that will Motivate You*

OLUSEGUN MARTINS

WESTBOW
PRESS®
A DIVISION OF THOMAS NELSON
& ZONDERVAN

WestBow Press books may be ordered through booksellers or by contacting:

WestBow Press
A Division of Thomas Nelson & Zondervan
1663 Liberty Drive
Bloomington, IN 47403
www.westbowpress.com
1 (866) 928-1240

Because of the dynamic nature of the Internet, any web addresses or links contained in this book may have changed since publication and may no longer be valid. The views expressed in this work are solely those of the author and do not necessarily reflect the views of the publisher, and the publisher hereby disclaims any responsibility for them.

Any people depicted in stock imagery provided by Thinkstock are models, and such images are being used for illustrative purposes only. Certain stock imagery © Thinkstock.

ISBN: 978-1-4908-7098-4 (sc)
ISBN: 978-1-4908-7100-4 (hc)
ISBN: 978-1-4908-7099-1 (e)

Library of Congress Control Number: 2015902959

Print information available on the last page.

WestBow Press rev. date: 09/03/2015

ACKNOWLEDGMENTS

To God be the Glory for the writing and publishing of this book. Special appreciation and gratitude to my lovely wife, Omowunmi Martins, who inspired and motivated me to begin to write....

Contents

INTRODUCTION

Writing this book is a major limestone in my life. I have always known that the Lord has potentiated me to be a writer or to write a book, but I did not believe that I could make it happen. I have resigned to the reclusion and cubicle of my limitation, mediocrity, and complacent attitude or mentality. Despite my theological education, I have thought that the ability to write a book only belongs to certain privileged people. I have considered myself to belong to the disadvantaged, the have-nots, the less privileged or unprivileged, and the minority group. But the motivation, inspiration, and grace to write this book has taught me that there is an excellent spirit in everybody. I have discovered that connection with God is a basis for distinction in life. To God be the glory!

But you may not understand all these preambles unless you know the story of my life. It is not a sweet story. It is a story that triggers some painful trauma as well as opens some healed wounds that have been buried in my subconscious and unconscious grave. Without this story I cannot boast of His glory in my life. The Lord has allowed me to be wounded, hounded, weakened, trashed, trampled upon, forgotten, abandoned, and despised in life. I am not saying all this to invoke your sympathy, empathy, pity, and compassion. I am only saying this to encourage, inspire, and motivate somebody.

Therefore, this is not my autobiography, but a devotional, inspirational, motivational didactic, and homiletical piece, that has helped me to get to where I am in life. However, a little bit of who I was and who I am has dovetailed the writing and contents of this book.

I was born healthy and hearty like every bouncing baby boy. I was doing well at school as a small boy in my primary school. All of a sudden something happened to me that changed the course of my life. I became seriously sick. Up till today, I do not know the nature or name of this sickness. There was no medical diagnosis and prognosis that provided any record about this sickness. All that I can say is that this sickness knocked me down and I was paralyzed for about fourteen months. I could not walk, stand, and do anything by myself. I became an invalid, totally paralyzed. But thank God for my mother who bore all the brunt of my uselessness, helplessness, and hopelessness. She continued to pray for me and paid for all kinds of physicians to provide care for me at home. Then I began to recover.

When I recovered, I lost the proper use of my right leg and left arm. The ugly results of my sickness redefined and re-described who I was. I felt that I had lost my identity. I could not go back to school. Not that I could not walk, but because of my new outlook. I became invisible. I developed pity for myself. I thought that was the end of my life. I lost hope in everything. I lost my friends at school. I lost my age mates. I lost my passion for anything. I lost hope in going forward in life.

Later on, the Lord made it possible for me to go back to school. I resumed primary 5 (5th grade). I was always afraid and shy to go to school. I thought that I was different from other students in the school. I felt that I was abnormal, a misnomer, and not fit to complete my education. But the grace of God kept me there. I finished and enrolled in junior high school. It was while I was in junior high school that I gave my life to the Lord and since that day, I began to experience the love of God and as well as His purpose for my life. At this time, I began to have the burden to work for the Lord as a full time minister. I would soon quit the junior high school to enter a 4-year Bible College. I knew that my purpose was in fulfilling God's purpose for my life.

While in the Bible College, God began to give me purpose, meaning, fulfillment, and passion for my life. During my third year in the Bible College, I took and sat for 5 subjects in General Certificate of Education (GCE equivalent of a GED). I passed 4, and failed English. When I graduated from the Bible College and posted to pastor a church, I re-took the English and had credit. I did not know why I was doing all this. It was not until after 7 years in the pastoral ministry that I was recommended and considered by the leaders of my denomination to be sponsored to a four-year degree program at one of the best seminaries in Nigeria, ECWA Theological Seminary (Evangelical Church Winning All), in Igbaja. I was admitted in 1990 and I graduated *cum laude* in 1994. After this, through the help of God and other people of God, I attended The Nigerian Baptist Theological Seminary where I graduated with a Master of Arts in Theological Studies.

I kept on doing the work of God passionately, sacrificially, dedicatedly, loyally, and wholeheartedly. Sometimes, the church could not pay my small and meager salaries for many months, but I kept on doing the work of God. My philosophy then was that, and still that, He that calls me is faithful and will do it. I believe that it is God who has called me, and if He has called me, then my life is in His hands. Therefore, I am not in the pastoral ministry because of money, but because of His calling upon my life. That, the Lord has not called me to be successful, but to be faithful and that there is no way I will be faithful and will not be successful.

As the Lord continued to show His faithfulness to me, He led me to my wife who is a citizen of Nigeria and America. She was serving as an active duty soldier in the US Army when the Lord brought us together providentially. After we got married, I joined her in Germany where she was stationed until she was reassigned and re-stationed back in the USA. From this time on, the story of my life began to change. While in the USA, I pursued another Master of Arts in Religion with a concentration in Pastoral Counseling at Liberty University (Lynchburg, VA) and graduated *cum laude*. I also pursued chaplaincy courses at Rhode Island Hospital (Providence, RI) and obtained a Clinical Pastoral Education (CPE) level 1. In 2010, I applied and was admitted to the Doctor of Ministry in Marriage and Family Counseling program at Gordon Conwell Theological Seminary. I have completed all the course work but still writing my final thesis project as at the time of writing this book.

Dear reader, you will know that I have every reason to have given up in life. I have every reason to give up on God, on myself, on people, and on my destiny. I cannot be where I am today if not for the grace and mercy of God. I am not claiming to be rich financially and materially, but I am rich spiritually and in the will of God for my life. The Lord has used me and is using me to impact and affect lives positively. The Lord has laid it on my heart to write this book, to educate, inspire, motivate, and encourage people. It is titled, *The Socio-Spiritual Recipes for Becoming Excellent in Life: Eleven Dynamic Keys that will Motivate You.*

The eleven chapters of this book are based on the socio-spiritual experience, conditions, and values that have helped me in life to be what I am, who I am, and where God has destined me to be. They are not compendiums or anecdotes of my life odyssey. They are rather biblical, social, and practical principles that have helped me and which I believe will help you in the journey of your life. They are meant to boost your socio-spiritual energy for excellence.

It is a devotional book. It is an inspirational book. It is a motivational book. It is a homiletical book. It is a didactic book. It is not a positive psychology book. It is a book that is hinged upon the revelation of the Word of God. It is a book that will guide, encourage, and help you to move from the attitude and mentality of defeat to overcome, loss to win, complacence to excellence, failure to success, disappointment to appointment, sinking to soaring, bitter to better, hopeless to hopeful, and so on. May the Lord bless you as you read this book. Amen.

Come on board as I share with you the eleven socio-spiritual recipes that God has taught me and also used to make me to become what I am and who I am, according to His purpose, and which I know will help you to become the excellent person that God has destined you to be. Happy reading!

Olusegun Martins (D. Min Candidate)

Chapter One

Recover from Your Losses

> *If you don't confront your fear, you will remain fearful in life. If you don't confront your failure, you will remain a failure in life. If you don't confront your disappointment, you will remain disappointed in life.*

The word "loss" means to suffer a defeat, a failure, a setback, a disappointment, a letdown or a negative outcome. A loss occurs when you experience destruction, a ruin, a defeat, a missed opportunity, and a back to zero. A loss may be emotional, psychological, physical, financial, vocational, and even spiritual. Loss is an unavoidable experience of life. Solomon in Ecclesiastes 3:1 & 6 says in the New King James Version: "To everything there is a season, A time for every purpose under heaven... A time to gain, And a time to lose..." This shows that loss is part of time. That you lose does not mean that God does not love you. That you lose does not mean that you are not a child of God. That you lose does not mean that you have reached the end of your life. That you lose is an indication that you are a candidate for recovery.

But what do you do when you lose that job? What do you do when you lose that opportunity? What do you do when you lose your peace? What do you do when you lose your connection with God? What do you do when you lose that relationship? What do you do when you lose that person in your life? What do you when you lose…? Elisabeth Kubler-Ross in her book *On Death and Dying* described five things which people do to handle losses. They are:

- **Denial** - "I feel fine.", "This can't be happening, not to me."
- **Anger** - "Why me? It's not fair!", "How can this happen to me?"
- **Bargaining** – "What can I do?", "I think I can still do something."
- **Depression** - "I'm so sad, why bother with anything?", "I don't want to do anything again." "I am tired."
- **Acceptance** - "It's going to be okay.", "I can't fight it.", "It is well."

David experienced a loss for the first time in his life. God used this to teach him a lesson, that life is not about winning alone, it is also about losing. You don't need success if you have never experienced failure because failure is success turned upside down. Failure is never final. Failure is not the end of the story. But how did he handle his loss and how can we handle our losses and recover from them? The following six "self" concepts are needed, based on the passage 1 Samuel 30: 1-10 & 17-20.

Self-Realization

When David and his men reached Ziklag, they found it destroyed
by fire and their wives and sons and daughters taken captive.
So David and his men wept aloud until they had no strength
left to weep. David's two wives had been captured – Ahinoam of
Jezreel and Abigail, the widow of Nabal of Carmel [vs. 3-5]

The first thing to be done is that you must realize the reality of what has happened or is happening to you. This is not the time to pretend or live in denial. Don't pretend by putting bandages and masks on your problems. There must be self-awareness or self-realization of your loss. You need to be able to honestly say that, "It is real; this is happening to me." The Bible says that David and his men wept aloud until they could weep no more. They openly expressed their feelings to one another. They knew that they had one thing in common: their wives and children had been taken captive. They have lost something. They suffered much loss.

This is the problem with many people. They act and behave as if they don't have any loss in their lives. They act and behave as if they are better than others. They act as if their lives are better, their marriages are better, their children are better, their spouses are better, their jobs are better, their finances are better, their spiritual lives are better, and that everything is better. They act as if spiritual people do not cry. They act as if it is unspiritual and unscriptural to have a problem. If you want to find out about the reality of losses in people as well as believers' lives, you will need to ask Job who lost all that he had; Abraham who lost Lot to the raiding kings; Apostle Paul who lost all his socio-religious achievements; and Jesus Christ who lost all to save us.

Brethren, I want you to know that **realization is the key to restoration. Unless you realize it you cannot overcome it. Unless you express it, you will regret it.**

Sometimes, Christianity has made people to live in denial and become hypocritical when it comes to the expression of emotion. We teach and preach to people to be strong and not weep, to be strong and not express feelings, to be strong and act as if nothing has happened to them. As a result, many are bleeding inside, but smiling outside; many are crying inside, but dancing outside. The church has developed everyone to become another "spiritual Robocop." I am not against faith or promoting sight (reality). But what I am saying is that, there is nothing wrong to express what we feel as humans. It is wrong to live in denial. Jesus did not deny the reality of the cross that was ahead of Him. The Bible says this about how He expressed His feelings in Mark 14:34 & 36: *"He told them, 'My soul is crushed with grief to the point of death. Stay here and keep watch with me…' 'Abba, Father,' he cried out, 'everything is possible for you. Please take this cup of suffering away from me. Yet I want your will to be done, not mine.'* (New Living Translation). Jesus realized the reality of what was about to happen to Him. He expressed His feelings.

Stop being a superman! Stop being an iron woman! Stop pretending to be invisible and immortal! You need to realize that you have a loss or losses in your life. You need to realize that you need the help of God. You need to realize that you need the help of people. You need to realize that you cannot help yourself. You cannot continue to cover up your problems and losses with church activities or spiritual exercises. You need to get real with yourself and with your life. David and the men with him got real with their conditions – their city had been destroyed and their children taken captive while they were on the battleground. The enemies came and ambushed them. The unexpected happened. Their winning team became the whining team.

All had been lost. At this point, David had nothing more to support himself. No one in Israel can help him. The Philistines did not want him. His family was gone; all that he owned was gone. But at least he has his friends, right? Not really, the people spoke of stoning him. Every support was gone, except the Lord. They could not deny the reality of the problem at hand. It was a great loss.

Jesus also wept when He saw the reality of the power of death and the sorrow that came on the family and friends of Lazarus after they lost him. Hear what the Bible says in John 11:33-35:

> [33] *"When Jesus saw her weeping, and the Jews who had come along with her also weeping, he was deeply moved in spirit*

4

*and troubled. * [34] *'Where have you laid him?' he asked. 'Come and see, Lord,' they replied.* [35] *Jesus wept."*

What is your loss? How are you handling your loss? Many people de-realized their losses by taking drugs to get high, attending and functioning in the church to diffuse the reality of their losses, going to nightclubs and partying, drinking alcohol, and putting on spiritual façade as if all is well. Many have never confessed or expressed to others that there is a loss in their lives. They look normal, but they are abnormal. They look restful, but they are restless. They look graceful, but they are disgraceful. Even our Lord Jesus Christ in the Garden of Gethsemane expressed the reality of His suffering as well as the cross was before Him to His disciples. Hear what He said: *"And He said to them, 'My soul is exceedingly sad (overwhelmed with grief) so that it almost kills Me! Remain here and keep awake and be watching.'"* [Mark 14:34, Amplified].

"He told them, 'My soul is crushed with grief to the point of death. Stay here and keep watch with me.' " [Mark 14:34, New Living Translation].

Jesus expressed the seriousness of His coming loss to His trusted friends and asked them to be praying for Him. This shows that it is not wrong for anyone to express his/her feelings either to God or to people. Expression is therapeutic. Expression is an antidote to depression. Therefore, you have to realize your loss by expressing it.

Self-Empowerment

David was greatly distressed because the men were talking of stoning him; each one was bitter in spirit because of his sons and daughters. But David found strength in the Lord his God [v.6]

One of the things that happens to us when we are going through losses is to lose inner strength and courage in ourselves, in others, and in God. This is what we call depression. The New English Translation (NET) Bible reads verse 6 as this, *"David was very upset, for the men were thinking of stoning him; each man grieved bitterly over his sons and daughters. But David drew strength from the Lord his God."*

Hear this, the problem is not what has happened to you, but how you are reacting to what has happened to you.

There are many people today who are very upset about something. David also was upset (in "distress" in the NIV). I have heard people use that phrase many times, "I am upset". Whenever you are upset, you will lose inner courage and strength in yourself and in God. Instead, you will begin to focus on your outward strength or energy on fighting somebody or some people whom you believe are the causes of the losses. Sometimes, we begin to project our anger on people: children, spouses, friends, colleagues, pastor, and even God. This was what the men with David were doing. We make people around us to feel the heat of the fire or problem that we are going through. They become the scapegoats or objects of our anger.

The Bible says that, *"the men were talking of stoning him."* How many people have you stoned verbally, emotionally, physically, psychologically, and spiritually because you are upset? Think of many people you have attacked verbally because of what you are going through. Think of many people you are attacking emotionally and psychologically because of what has happened to you. Think about the many people who have become victims of your physical attacks as a result of that loss that happened in your life. Think about what you have damaged by your words and actions because of that thing that happened to you. Think... *What are you doing with that stone... ?*

Why did they have to stone David? He also had lost wives and children. He also has a lot of losses. Why did they have to make that person the object of their anger as a result of what they were going through? Don't you know that everybody also goes through "losses?" Is it because he or she is dancing and praising the Lord? He or she also have many losses. Why are you adding more losses to another person's losses because of your losses? Why do you have to stone that David? You are not the only person with problems. You are not the only person with losses. *YOU DON'T NEED TO HURT PEOPLE BECAUSE YOU ARE HURT*. Instead, deal with your hurt as David dealt with his. How?

The Bible says that, *"But David drew strength from the Lord his God"* [NIV]. What does that mean? It means that he did not waste his time and energy on fighting people; rather he sought for strength from God to handle the problem. What you need is not the power to run away from the problem or to fight back, but you need power to cope when you are under stress. This is what David is saying, "I don't need stones, but I need God;" "I don't need to lose my mind, I need the peace of God;" "I don't need to solve it with my own power, I need the power of God."

Let me tell you this, you can never solve any problems in your life or recover any losses in your life by your own power. No wonder the Bible says in Isaiah 30:15, *"This is what the Sovereign Lord, the Holy One of Israel, says: 'In repentance and rest is your salvation, in quietness and trust is your strength' "*. Unless you empower yourself in the strength of God you will always remain defeated and in total loss every time. If you allow your problem to overpower you, then you can never overcome the problem. Any time you lose courage, you have lost it. You need to be encouraged and empowered in yourself in the Lord. Hear what Solomon says in Proverb 24:10: *"If you **falter** in a time of trouble, how small is your strength!"* The New Living Translation says, *"If you fail under pressure, your strength is too small."* There is nothing that happens to you that is beyond your God's given capacity. That is why He said in 1 Corinthians 10:13: *"No temptation has overtaken you except what is common to mankind. And God is faithful; he will not let you be* *tempted beyond what you can bear. But when you are tempted, he will also provide a way out so that you can endure it".* I love the way the Amplified Bible puts it below:

> *"For no temptation (no trial regarded as enticing to sin), [no matter how it comes or where it leads] has overtaken you and laid hold on you that is not common to man [that is, no temptation or trial has come to you that is beyond human resistance and that is not adjusted and adapted and belonging to human experience, and such as man can bear]. But God is faithful [to His Word and to His compassionate nature], and He [can be trusted] not to let you be tempted and tried and assayed beyond your ability and strength of resistance and power to endure, but with the temptation He will [always] also provide the way out (the means of escape to a landing place), that you may be capable and strong and powerful to bear up under it patiently."*

This verse shows that you have the capacity to handle the calamity that has come over your life if you can empower yourself through the strength of God. That is, you have to rely on God and derive your coping strength from Him.

How do you react to things? How do you handle your losses? What types of actions and attitudes do you put on when you are experiencing losses? Are you offensive, defensive, combative, or sarcastic? It is better to use that energy or power to build yourself up for recovery. What are you doing with that stone? Remember Isaiah 40:31:

> *"But those who wait for the Lord [who expect, look for, and hope in Him] shall change and renew their strength and power; they shall lift their wings and mount up [close to God] as eagles [mount up to the sun]; they shall run and not be weary, they shall walk and not faint or become tired."* [Amplified].

Self-Focus

Then David said to Abiathar the priest, the son of Ahimelek,
"Bring me the ephod." Abiathar brought it to him [v.7]

David might have lost his city, his wives, and children, but He did not lose his focus on God. David said: let the devil take everything, my joy, my hope, my pride, my home, my health, my dreams, my possession, my future, and my all, but one thing is certain, he cannot take my focus on God.

Many people have lost focus on God because of what has happened to them as well as what they are going through. Many are saying, "God, give me a break, when I am ok I will come back to you." In fact, many people will prefer to lose God than to lose all those things.

Even though Job lost all, but he did not lose God. Even when his wife told him to disown God so that she could stand by him, he refused. R. Miller wrote a Hymn titled **I'd Rather Have Jesus,** below are the lyrics of the hymn:

I'd rather have Jesus than silver or gold;
I'd rather be His than have riches untold;
I'd rather have Jesus than houses or lands;
I'd rather be led by His nail-pierced hand

I'd rather have Jesus than men's applause;
I'd rather be faithful to His dear cause;
I'd rather have Jesus than worldwide fame;
I'd rather be true to His holy name

When things go tough and rough, who and what is your focus? Or now that you are going through that thing in your life, what and who is your focus? Where is the place of God in your crisis? Sometimes God allows you to lose some things in life instead of losing Him in your life. If God is to be your focus, all other things that would take His place must be lost. That is why Paul said, "I counted it as loss all those things that are supposed to be a gain to me."

Let us see what David did and his focus when he suffered the greatest loss in his life. The Bible says, "*Then David said to Abiathar the priest, the son of Ahimelek, "Bring me the ephod." Abiathar brought it to him, 8 and David inquired of the Lord*".

When others are bringing stones of attack, stones of offence, stone of defense and stones of defiance, David asked for the 'stone of help', the rock of ages, the stone of Zion. He asked for the Ephod. He asked for God. He knew that this was the time to focus on God. This was the time he needed God more. I don't know what you are going through in your life, but this is the time to come closer to God. The Ephod in the Old Testament was the mantic or cultic means of communicating with God. David is saying: "Give me God so that I can give Him my problem." Who are you giving your problem to?

Many people think that hating God, abandoning God, running away from God, abusing God, and even cursing God is the best thing to do when things become rough and tough. God is not and will never be the cause of any problem in our lives. God is a good God and does what is always good. God did not kill your son, your daughter, your child, your wife, your husband, your parents, your fiancé, your fiancée, your best friend, and your co-worker. It is not God. God did not cause you to lose your job, your house, and even your marriage. God may PERMIT it for a purpose, but He did not CAUSE it to happen. I want you to reflect on these two words: **permit** and **cause**. To permit means to allow to do something, to allow to be done or occur, to allow the doing of something. To cause, on the other hand denotes a person or thing that acts, happens, or exists in such a way that some specific thing happens as a result, the producer of an effect. The Division of Motor Vehicle (DMV) may permit or approve you to drive by giving you driver's license, but they are not responsible or the cause of any accident you have. Sometimes we blame the wrong person, God.

One of the best ways to recover from loss or losses is to focus on God. That is when you need God most. If you focus on the problem, you will see the bigness of the problem. But if you focus on God, you will see the smallness of the problem. When you focus on your problem God will become too small in your eyes to trust, but when you focus on God, your problem will become too small in your eyes. David was able to defeat his Goliath because he focused on God. Peter was able to walk on his stormy sea because he focused on Jesus. Recovery is all about focus. No wonder David said in Psalms 16:8: *"I have set the Lord continually before me; because He is at my right hand, I shall not be moved"* [Amplified]. The writer of Hebrews also encourages everyone that is going through tough and rough times in the following words:

> *"Therefore, since we are surrounded by such a great cloud of witnesses, let us throw off everything that hinders and the sin that so easily entangles. And let us run with perseverance the race marked out for us, fixing our eyes on Jesus, the pioneer and perfecter of faith. For the joy set before him he endured the cross, scorning its shame, and sat down at the right hand of the throne of God"* [Hebrews 12:1-2].

What have you lost in your life that is greater than God?

Self-Responsibility

8 So David inquired of the Lord, saying, "Shall I pursue this troop? Shall I overtake them?" And He answered him, "Pursue, for you shall surely overtake them and without fail recover all."9 So David went, he and the six hundred men who were with him, and came to the Brook Besor, where those stayed who were left behind. 10 But David pursued, he and four hundred men; for two hundred stayed behind, who were so weary that they could not cross the Brook Besor. [vs. 8-10, NKJV].

There is something interesting in these three verses (8-10). They are verbs, words of action. In verse 8 we see the word "inquired", verse 9 the word "went" and verse 10 we have the word "pursued." And these verses reveal that David was the one performing the actions of these verbs. In other words, David *inquired, went,* and *pursued.* This is what I call, taking responsibility.

It takes a responsible person to take responsibility for his or her actions. We love to play the blame game by making excuses and shifting responsibilities. We love to say, "It is not me;" "It is not my fault;" "I don't know anything about it;" or "It is the devil." It all began with Adam in the Garden of Eden. He refused to take responsibility for his action; he blamed the woman. This is what people do during conflicts, crises, and losses. They play blame others. Many are playing the roles of innocents by developing what we call "Victim Mentality." They refuse to acknowledge that they are also responsible. Unless you accept responsibility for your problem you will never get out of the problem.

Whether we know it, or not, most of us react to life as victims. Whenever we refuse to take responsibility for ourselves, we are unconsciously choosing to react as the victim. Then we will begin to play the three roles in the Karpman Drama Triangle for victim mentality. They are: **Rescuer Persecutor,** and **Victim.**

> **The Rescuers** see themselves as "helpers" and "caretakers."

> **The Persecutors** identify themselves primarily as victims in need of protection.

The Victims believe they cannot take care of themselves, but need somebody to take care of them.

To be free from your problem, you have to set yourself free. You must know how to get away from Victim Mentality by taking RESPONSIBILITY. This is what David did. This is what distinguishes a winner from a loser, a victor from a victim, and an overcomer from a defeated person. You have to own your problem. You have to see yourself as one of the contributors to your problem. Don't blame your spouse, your parents, your friends, your colleagues, your bosses, and everyone for what has happened to you. It takes two to tango. You have to do what David did. What did David do?

He inquired from the Lord on what to be done [v.8]. He could have told the priests or the prophets to do that for him. He could have shifted his responsibility because he has lost his children and family by blaming either God or others. But he did not. He took action. He decided to take the bull by the horns. He did not make the mistake which he made before by not asking from God; he took time to inquire from the Lord. Unless God directs you, you can never recover your loss. **Unless God recover it, you cannot discover it.**

But wait a minute! From whom do you inquire about your life? Who is your guide? Many people think that they don't need God when they are making a serious decision in their life. Many people don't even know how to inquire from God. Remember that God knows all things. He knows all things about your past, present, and future. He sees more than you can see. He can see the end from the beginning. He can see clearer and better than you. That is why you need His daily guide. You need to find out from Him before embarking on that thing. Hear what Solomon says in Proverbs 16:1&9: *"To humans belong the plans of the heart, but from the Lord comes the proper answer of the tongue. In their hearts*

13

humans plan their course, but the Lord establishes their steps." Do not leave God how of your plans.

He went after the people who had taken his wife and children [v.9]. Because he took the responsibility to go, others followed him. If he had remained there weeping and crying, nothing would be recovered. Worrying, whining, blaming, complaining, and making excuses for your loss and failure cannot amount to anything in your life. You have to go after it. Listen to this: **Any problem that you run away from will always be there in your life.** Life is never without a problem or a loss, but you don't make them to become your master. Don't allow any loss or problem in your life to keep you from moving forward in life. If you don't go after it, you will never recover it.

He pursued the captors (v.10). He refused to let them take his wife, his children, and the family of his soldiers. I want you to know this; **the devil will not give up if you give up, but the devil will give up if you don't give up.** You don't run from your problems. David knew the secret of not running away from one's problems and challenges. He did not run away from the bears and lions that came to steal the sheep which he was taking care of in the field. He fought them and took his sheep back (1 Samuel 17:34-37). He did not run away from the intimidation of Goliath. When others ran away, he pursued him (1 Samuel 17:43-50). The only person that he avoided, not running away from, was King Saul. Not that he was afraid of him, but he did not want to kill him. David knew that the best solution to every problem, fear, failure, and loss is to confront it. **If you don't confront your fear, you will remain fearful in life. If you don't confront your failure, you will remain a failure in life. If you don't confront your disappointment, you will remain disappointed in life.**

You can take it back. You can take your joy back. Stop crying. Stop complaining. Take actions. When? Now.

Self-Efforts

¹⁷"David fought them from dusk until the evening of the next day, and none of them got away, except four hundred young men who rode off on camels and fled. ¹⁸David recovered everything the Amalekites had taken, including his two wives. ¹⁹Nothing was missing: young or old, boy or girl, plunder or anything else they had taken. David brought everything back. ²⁰He took all the flocks and herds, and his men drove them ahead of the other livestock, saying, 'This is David's plunder' " [vs. 17-20]

From verses 1-31 of this chapter, the name of David is repeated 27 times. In verses 17-20 some actions were credited to David. For instance,

- In verse 17, David attacked them;
- In verse 18 & 19, David recovered all;
- In verse 20, David took all.

David did not sit there wishing and praying that all their losses would be recovered. Instead, he attacked, he recovered, and he took. That you have waited on the Lord in prayers does not mean that you should not go out and do your part. God will not go out for you, but He will only go out with you. That is why He has given you your legs, your arms, your brains, your eyes, and your will so that you can act in faith. Unless you put your faith into action, you will remain defeated in life.

If David had refused to take it upon himself to go out and attack and recover them, the captives would remain there as captives. Unless you take steps and efforts you will never know that God can help you. In fact in life, **you have to do all what you can and allow God to do all what you can't. And if you remain in the same place, you will be in shame.**

Remember that David did not go by information or divination, but he acted by revelation and faith. The problem with many Christians and people today is that they are pursuing their losses without God and they have never recovered. You must learn to commit your ways into the hands of the Lord and He will direct your paths. Like David, many people only remember to commit to God their problems, losses, failures, and trials. This is the only time when they remember God. There is no problem with this. However, you must know that **God can do all things only if you are willing to do something**. God's doing all things is always contingent on your doing something.

- Abraham must go with his soldiers to fight those who have taken Lot as prisoner before he could recover him and all his goods (Genesis 14:11-16)
- Isaac must plant in that land before he could recover from the famine that came upon the land (Genesis 26:12-14)
- Isaac must dig all the closed wells before he could experience Rehoboth (Genesis 26:22)
- Jacob must negotiate his contract with his father in law before he could recover all his wasted years (Genesis 30:23-ff)
- Naomi must go back to Bethlehem before she could recover from all her losses (Ruth 1:6)
- The poor widow of a prophet must borrow pots in order to recover from her debts (2 Kings 4:1-7)
- The son of the prophet must cry to Elisha and reach out his hand to recover back the lost axe head (2 Kings 6:1-7)
- The servants at the marriage in Cana of Galilee must pour water into the empty pots before they could recover from the finished wine (John 2:11)

Brethren, you can if you will. Remember this,

- God can turn your captivity to ability
- God can turn your calamity to stability
- God can turn your adversity to celebrity
- God can turn your scarcity to opportunity

Only if you are willing to take actions... Go out there and attack, recover, and take back all that the devil has stolen from you. Unless you go, you can never recover. The Lord has answered your prayers, but you need to go and recover your all...

Self-Selflessness

21 "Then David came to the two hundred men who had been too exhausted to follow him and who were left behind at the Besor Valley. They came out to meet David and the men with him. As David and his men approached, he asked them how they were. 22 But all the evil men and troublemakers among David's followers said, 'Because they did not go out with us, we will not share with them the plunder we recovered. However, each man may take his wife and children and go.' 23 David replied, 'No, my brothers, you must not do that with what the Lord has given us. He has protected us and delivered into our hands the raiding party that came against us. 24 Who will listen to what you say? The share of the man who stayed with the supplies is to be the same as that of him who went down to the battle. All will share alike.' 25 David made this a statute and ordinance for Israel from that day to this. 26 When David reached Ziklag, he sent some of the plunder to the elders of Judah, who were his friends, saying, 'Here is a gift for you from the plunder of the Lord's enemies' " [vs. 21-26]

This is more or else an outcome rather than prerequisite. It was after David recovered all his losses that he developed the sense of self-selflessness. To be selfless is to be unselfish. One can decide to be stingy and selfish as a result of what he or she has gone through in life. This is what David's friends did. Verse 22 says that they objected to sharing part of the spoil or excess of things recovered with those who refused to go with them to the battle. They did not want to share the proceeds from their sweat or labor with others. Sometimes, many of us act like this. We think that we have acquired back or recovered or gotten all that we have through our might and strength. Often times we forget God, and we also forget people around us. The Lord warned the children of Israel against this in Deuteronomy 8:17-19:

> *[17]" And beware lest you say in your [mind and] heart, My power and the might of my hand have gotten me this wealth. [18] But you shall [earnestly] remember the Lord your God, for it is He Who gives you power to get wealth, that He may establish His covenant which He swore to your fathers, as it is this day. [19] And if you forget the Lord your God and walk after other gods and serve them and worship them, I testify against you this day that you shall surely perish"* [Amplified].

Brethren, think about all what you have gone through in life. Think about all the losses, failures, setbacks, disappointments, and calamities that you have experienced in your life. Also think about all your struggles for survival and how you have gotten to where you are now. What should you do? I think you should do as David did, give to the Lord and to others (v.26). I know that day, David remembered the priests of God, the prophets of God, the Levites of God, and all the elders or older men in the city who could not go with them to share with them what the Lord has done for them.

When you recover don't cover up, but uncover it. Don't hide your testimony. Don't hide your miracle. Don't hide your success. Don't hide your restoration. Don't hide the goodness of God in your life. Don't hide your recovery. Don't monopolize or marginalize what God has done in your life, publicize it.

What have you done with your recovery? What are you doing with your recovery? What are you going to do with your recovery?

- When Abraham recovered, he paid his tithe. (Genesis 14:17-20)
- When Jacob recovered, he went back to Bethel where he had made a vow to the Lord. (Genesis 31:13; 35:1,3-15)
- When David recovered, he promised to give back to the Lord. (Psalms 116:12-19)
- When Hezekiah recovered, he composed and sang a song to the Lord. (Isaiah 38:9-20)
- When Job recovered from all his losses he organized a celebration for his friends and acquaintances. (Job 42:10-11).
- When Jesus resurrected and defeated the devil, He appeared and fellowshipped with His followers.

It does not matter all what you have lost or the loss in your life, or how long it has been; you can recover all through the help of the Lord. All you have to do is take the above-mentioned practical steps. Do not mourn your life; celebrate it. Do not give up on yourself; pursue it. It is never too late for you to recover all that the devil has stolen in your life. You can recover from your defeat. You can recover from your failure. You recover from your setback. You can recover from your disappointment. You can recover from your sickness. You can recover from... - just name it. You will recover back in Jesus' name.

CHAPTER TWO

You Have to Take Steps To Becoming Better in Life

You cannot be bitter and better.....
and cannot be better and bitter

There always comes a point in time when one will be fed up and tired of routine and doing the same stuff. Being in the same position or situation for a long time will make you dormant, hopeless, helpless, purposeless, dreamless, myopic, traditional and conservative. The Lord has not created us to be in this kind of state. Rather, He wants us to become better in life. That is, the Lord wants us to become better than what we are and move from where we are right now.

Our Lord Jesus Christ, when He was on Earth, spent time to provide better things for people and to make their lives better as well. No one encountered Jesus and remained the same. They always got better and became their best. He came to deliver them from not only the power of sin, but also from the old and legalistic tradition of Moses. That was why all the miracles He performed were contrary to the tradition of Moses. All His miracles were proofs of better things. They all broke protocols, traditions, rules, regulations, because they are better things. That is what God wants for us in this life, to become better every day, every week, every month, every year, and every moment. From the passage, John 5:1-9, we shall examine six keys to becoming your better in life.

Expectation

"In these lay a great multitude of sick people, blind, lame, paralyzed, waiting for the moving of the water" (v. 3, NKJV).

This is the first key to becoming better in life. It is called expectation. The word "expectation" means to hope for and anticipate in something. That is, to believe that something good or better will happen. This is one of the definitions of faith in Hebrew 11:1, "Now faith is being sure of what we hope for and certain of what we do not see." Sometimes faith is an act of expectation - believing that it will happen.

In verse 3 of our text, the Bible says, *"In these lay a great multitude of sick people, blind, lame, paralyzed, waiting for the moving of the water"* (NKJV).

These people, despite their hopeless condition and social isolation, the Bible says that they were still, *"waiting for the moving of the water."* The moving of the water was the only hope that they had. They were all there every year waiting for the moving of the water. They were expecting. They did not give up on God. They did not give up on themselves. They did not give up on the solution. They did not become bitter and were expecting to become better. They stayed there hoping. For how long can you stay there, *"waiting for the moving of the water?"*

What is the importance of *"the moving of the water?"* The moving of the water, once in a year, is God's solution to their expectation.

Despite their hopeless situations, these invalid and sick people still had hope in the moving water. They knew that God had not forgotten them. They knew even though society, friends, families, and even colleagues had forgotten them or written them off, but God has not. No wonder they stayed and remained in that place, called Bethesda, the house of mercy, waiting for the mercy of God. How long could they wait for the moving of the water? They did not know the day, month, and time when the angel of the Lord would come and move the water…, but they were all expecting. For how long have you been waiting and expecting? Your water of solution, your water of mercy, your water of blessing, your water of help is going to be moved one day. Just don't give up expecting. Don't give up your expectation. Hear what Hebrews 10:35-39 says:

> [35] *"So do not throw away your confidence; it will be richly rewarded.*
>
> [36] *You need to persevere so that when you have done the will of God, you will receive what he has promised.* [37] *For, 'In just a little while, he who is coming will come and will not delay.'* [38] *And, 'But my righteous one will live by faith. And I take no pleasure in the one who shrinks back.'* [39] *But we do not belong to those who shrink back and are destroyed, but to those who have faith and are saved."*

Many people have given up in themselves. They have written off themselves. They have stopped hoping for the best in life. They do not have any expectation that things will be better or best for them again. Instead of faith, they have resorted to fate. They have confined themselves to their situations and conditions. Many have developed a defeated mentality. These paralytic men did not. They still hoped for best. They hoped beyond hope. This is what God is expecting from everyone, hoping beyond your hopeless situation. Do not let your situation kill your expectation. The worst the situation, the greater the expectation should be. Always remember that God will not do it if you don't expect it.

The Lord wants you to come to the throne of His mercy where His mercy abounds for us all. Just like these paralyzed people, you must realize that you are powerless and incapable of helping yourself and unable to solve your problems. Hence, you must put aside all your pride and arrogance. You must come to the mercy of God with great expectation, believing that He can cause the water to move for our advantage. Hear what He says, *"For he says, 'In the time of my favor I heard you, and in the day of salvation I helped you.' I tell you, now is the time of God's favor, now is the day of salvation* (2 Cor. 6:2). Do not give up on God or on yourself. Keep on hoping. Keep on believing. To become better in life you must keep on expecting because...

- Expectation is the key to realization
- Expectation is the key to manifestation
- Expectation is the key to solution
- Expectation is the key to intervention
- Expectation is the key to visitation
- Expectation is the key to appropriation
- Expectation is the key to confirmation
- Expectation is key to possession
- Expectation is the key to allocation
- Expectation is the key to relocation

Aspiration

"Then whoever stepped in first, after the stirring of the water, was made well of whatever disease he had"[v. 4c, NKJV]

Here we are going to rearrange the verse starting from the cause to effect. That is, from motive to action or purpose to process. The rationale behind their stepping into the water was to be made well. This is called aspiration. The word aspiration means to have strong desire, longing, aim and ambition.

Note this: these invalid guys did not allow their various conditions to stop them from aspiring. They wished to become better. They wished for better in life. They refused to let their past and present condition cripple their future condition. They refused to be tagged as statistics. They hoped for the best. They hoped to become better. No wonder they struggled to get into the water. Their mindset was, "If I can just make it to the mowing water." They were tenacious. They moved from expectation to aspiration. They wanted to get better. They refused to be in the down low in life. They aspired for the better.

These sick men were persistent, consistent, and willing to be healed. Since nobody knew the day, week, month, and time when the moving of the water would take place, then, the person to be healed MUST have great aspiration.

Many people have allowed their conditions to kill their aspirations. They have stopped dreaming better dreams. They have stopped pursuing their dreams. They have given up by resorting to fate. They have resorted to be where they are because they have lost every will to aspire. Have you allowed your situation to kill your aspiration? If you do, you will become a statistic in life. You have to get up and move closer to the pool. You don't know when it is going to be your turn. Your moving water is God's opportunity for your life. Your moving water is what God wants to use to better your life. Get up and step into it. Stop praying about it. Step into it. Unless you step in by faith you can never become better in life.

If you don't aspire you will expire

These sick men did not look at how long they had been there. They did not look at who has gone ahead of them. They did not look at their inability to get into the pool when the angel came down to move the water years ago. They just kept on aspiring that one day they would become better. They were saying to themselves just as David said in Psalms 30:5[b]: *"Weeping may endure for a night, but joy comes in the morning."* [Amplified].

Aspiration made them to put their minds on the result rather than the insult, output rather than the input, end rather than the means. It is "aspiration" that will make you see beyond the present to the future. Aspiration will make you focus on what you will become rather than what has become of you. These men were able to see beyond their disabilities to their abilities. They knew they could become better. They refused to be defeated. You can get better if you aspire...

Perspiration

"For an angel went down at a certain time into the pool and stirred up the water; then whoever stepped in first, after the stirring of the water, was made well of whatever disease he had" (v. 4b, NKJV).

I want you to pay attention to this verse 4 properly. These sick people did not stop at aspiration. They took another step of perspiration. Listen to part b of verse 4, *"then whoever stepped in first, after the stirring of the water."* They did not wait for the angel of God to pour the water on them or to carry them into the water. Not at all. Instead, they all perspired or struggled to step in into the water. These invalid guys had nobody to carry them because they were all sick with problems. However, the only person who would get his healing after the moving of the water was the one who would first step in into the water. It was the survival of the fittest.

Perspiration is to take steps. The word "perspiration" means to perspire. To perspire means to sweat, to struggle, or to work hard. Just think of the process these sick people went through to get near the pool every year. There were no wheel chairs, no hoover around chairs, and no lifters. They had been abandoned in this nursing home called Bethesda. The name Bethesda means "House of Mercy." Even though they were at the House of Mercy, however, they must take steps to receiving this mercy.

Many people think that mercy of God is equal to doing nothing in life. It is not so. The mercy of God is not for the lazy, complacent, and docile people. The mercy of God is for those who can appropriate it and position themselves to receiving it. David received the mercy of God while he was in the wilderness being busy taking care of his father's business. Bartimeaus, the blind man, received the mercy of God when he was at the roadside begging for money. Do you know that you can be in the house of mercy and not receive mercy? Why? It is because you have refused to perspire or put in efforts. At least they struggled to step into the water by themselves. Unless you step in nothing will happen.

Naman the leper was told to immerse himself into the water seven times before he would be healed. He had to do something for something to happen. This is perspiration. Thank God that he did not quit when he wanted to quit. He would have remained a leper for life. Sometimes you have to go down if you want to go up in life. Sometimes you have to become sweat so that sweet can come out of your life. Sometimes you have to go through the pain so that gain will come. You have to perspire. Someone said: *"If you desire to acquire what you aspire in life, do not retire but refire."* To refire is to perspire. It is to put in little efforts. You are getting closer to the pool than you think. Keep on perspiring...

Determination

> *⁵"One who was there had been an invalid for thirty-eight years. ⁶When Jesus saw him lying there and learned that he had been in this condition for a long time, he asked him, 'Do you want to get well?'" [v. 5-6]*

Verses 5 and 6 introduces us to a particular man in this place. Verse 5 says: "*Now a certain man was there who had an infirmity thirty-eight years.*" This man had been there with his long and chronic problem. He had been there for a long time with his long problem. Verse 6 says: "*When Jesus saw him lying there, and knew that he already had been in that condition a long time, He said to him, 'Do you want to be made well?' *"

This man had been there for the past thirty-eight years. All those years, wasted! He had been there incapacitated and unable to do anything. Thirty-eight years? Yes. He was lying there helpless and hopeless. Even Jesus saw him there and knew that he had been there for a long time. What was he doing here? Why didn't he request to be taken home? Why was he wasting his time and efforts? It was because of one reason: DETERMINATION.

- Determination keeps you going
- Determination keeps you focus
- Determination keeps you hopeful
- Determination keeps you expecting
- Determination keeps you aspiring
- Determination keeps you perspiring
- Determination keeps you undoubting
- Determination keeps you unwavering
- Determination keeps you unrelenting
- Determination keeps you dreaming
- Determination keeps you believing

Here is the truth about this man. Even though he had been in this condition and situation for a long time, he did not give up waiting for when his turn would come to step into the water. He determined to wait for God's help and God's mercy. He did not move from one nursing home to another. He did not move from one church to another. He did not move from one marriage to another. He did not move from one business to another. He did not move from one ministry to another. He did not move from one relationship to another. He was determined to wait on the Lord. Even when his waiting did not make sense, he determined to wait. Even when people were laughing at him, he determined to wait. Even when people were mocking him, he determined to wait. Even when he thought nobody could help him, he determined to wait. Even when he thought nobody was with him, he determined to wait.

God always rewards determination. God is looking for those who will say like Job that, *"Though he **slay** me, yet will I hope in him; I will surely defend my ways to his face"* [Job 13:15]. And hear again what Job says about determination: *"If a man dies, will he live again? All the days of my hard service I will **wait** for my renewal to come"* [Job 14:14].

Many people lack determination today. They did not have the determination to wait for the Lord's time. They are in hurry and in desperation. They fail to realize that *desperation is the mother of frustration.* Their determination is in the opposite. It is determination to have it in their way and not in God's way. It is a lying and crooked kind of determination. But I am talking about determination to wait and still hope in God even when those you met at the pool have received their miracles. I am talking about determination that says, *"I lift up my eyes to you, to you whose throne is in heaven. As the eyes of slaves look to the hand of their master, as the eyes of a maid look to the hand of her mistress, so our eyes look to the LORD our God, till he shows us his mercy"* (Psalms 123:1-2). It is determination to become better even if your life, your marriage, your business, your relationship, your ministry has become bitter.

Motivation

*"Sir," the invalid replied, "I have no one to help me into
the pool when the water is stirred. While I am trying to
get in, someone else goes down ahead of me." [v. 7]*

In verse 7, this man gave an honest answer to Jesus' question in verse 6: *"When Jesus saw him lying there and learned that he had been in this condition for a long time, he asked him, 'Do you want to get well?' "* To this he answered, *'Sir, when the water is stirred, I don't have anybody to put me in the pool. By the time I get there, somebody else is already in' "* (The Message Bible). What a terrible situation. He could not walk and sit. He was completely paralyzed and incapacitated. But yet, he was at the pool. I thought before that he was making an excuse. No. He was stating a fact. Even though he was physically incapacitated, but he was psychologically motivated. Here is what he says, *"By the time I get there,* somebody else is already in." Wow! What a motivated man. He continued to motivate himself despite the fact that he had nobody to help him. Listen, **you don't need nobody, you need yourself.** Unless you help yourself, nobody will help you.

The man said, even though I don't have the connection, the ability, and the qualification, but I have one thing, MOTIVATION. He is saying, sir, I have the inner strength. I have the inner power. I have the inner energy. Sir, I may be defeated physically, but I am not defeated psychologically and emotionally. Thus far I have carried myself. I will get into the pool one day. It may be long, but I will get into the pool one day. It may look impossible, but I will get inside the pool one day. What a great motivation. In psychology, **motivation** refers to the initiation, direction, intensity, and persistence of behavior. It involves having the desire and willingness to do something.

Listen to me, if you don't encourage yourself, nobody will. If you don't motivate yourself, nobody will. If you don't move yourself, nobody will. You will remain there and continue to give stories and excuses of why you remain where you are. To get better in life, you need motivation and not frustration.

Action

Then Jesus said to him, 'Get up! Pick up your mat and walk.' 9
At once the man was cured; he picked up his mat and walked.
The day on which this took place was a Sabbath' " [vs. 8-9]

In response to his motivation, Jesus gave him a command in verses 8-9, *"Jesus said, 'Get up, take your bedroll, start walking.' The man was healed on the spot. He picked up his bedroll and walked off. That day happened to be the Sabbath."*

These are very interesting verses. This man received and became better in life through his response to Jesus' command. There were three active things he was commanded to do:

- He was to get up
- He was to pick up his mat
- He was to start walking

Brethren, you have to get up from that bed, couch or sofa of comfortability, idleness, complaint, complacency, mediocrity, and stagnancy. You have to get up and better your life. Sitting there with bitterness and self-pity will never help you. You cannot be bitter and get better. Get up! The same thing God said to Elijah when he was depressed. Get up! Tell yourself: get up!

Secondly, you have to break all the traditions, myths, and superstitions surrounding your situation by picking your mat or bedroll. Do not let that superstitious mentality tie you down in life. To this man, it was the Sabbath. No one was to take up his mat on the Sabbath. Taking up of the mat was considered a work and a violation of the Sabbath law. Sometimes, you have to break certain traditions and protocols if you want to get better in life. You don't have to worry about what people will say or are saying about the steps you are taking. You will have to take your mat or bedroll. Sometimes you step on toes to get better. You will have to break away from your familiar mat, the familiar habits, familiar friends, and familiar ways of life to the unfamiliar.

Finally, you must be ready to start walking even if you have never walked before. That is, you have to attempt to do the difficult if you want to be better in life. You must be ready to go through pain before you can have great gain in life. Sometimes you have to crawl if you cannot walk, stagger if you cannot walk, and keep on trying until you are on your feet again. You can become better in life...

Dear readers, it is the will of God for you to become better in life. However, God will not dump it on you. Not at all. You are responsible to making yourself better in life. Sometimes life is not about...

- Duration but the destination
- Age but the stage
- Makeup but the end-up
- Tragedy but the strategy
- Story but the glory

CHAPTER THREE

Demonstrate The Spiritual-Practical Formula For Success

"If you don't Discover Yourself, you will remain Covered in Life"

Philippians 4:13 has become a popular jingle for Christians and non-Christians alike. People have made stickers and fliers out of it. Many have memorized and confessed it. But only few have taken time to explore what it means and how it relates to success. The verse has been reduced to one of the motivational mantra that people chant as they are about to embark on something serious. The verse is more than this. This verse is a categorical statement from an apostle who was imprisoned, but who believed that his imprisonment was never a barrier to his achievement. That is what we want to explore in this message. We want to explore and examine Apostle Paul's spiritual as well as practical formula to becoming successful in life: *"I can do all things through Christ who strengthens me"* (New King James Version).

Why is this topic or subject necessary? It is necessary because success is not just conferred; it is earned. And you cannot earn it unless you motivate yourself. How can you motivate yourself?

It is not only through motivational books, speakers, and jingles, but through the six practical and spiritual truths which Paul mentions in this verse, Philippians 4:13 which says, *"I can do all things through Christ who strengthens me"* [NKJV]. What are they?

Believe in Yourself

"I"

The first word in this verse is the word "I." The word "I" is a powerful word. It is a word of emphasis, particularity and peculiarity. The Greek word for "I" is *"ego."* A famous psychologist by the name Sigmund Freud has described ego as the executive of the human personality that controls the gateways to action. Ego is the human self-confidence, self-sufficient, and self-ability. The use of the word "I" depicts confidence in oneself or belief in oneself even if no one does. This is not self-assertion, self-will and self-aggrandizement. Paul believes in himself even if no one believes in him.

The word "I" shows the power of the "you" that is in "you." Nobody can make you become anything in life unless you believe in yourself. It is you who can make you successful in life. It is not the system; it is not the program; it is not the career; and it is not the educational institution; IT IS YOU. It is you who can make things happen in your life. Unless you recognize yourself, you cannot believe in yourself. You are who you are. Nobody can be you. You cannot be somebody. You are unique. You are particular. You are peculiar. You were created to create…to make it…to be successful. But you must believe in yourself. That is, success will not come if you do not believe in yourself. You cannot succeed in life if you continue to doubt yourself.

You don't need peoples' approval before you will believe in yourself. You don't need peoples' acceptance before you can accept yourself. If you don't believe in yourself nobody will believe in you. If you don't accept yourself nobody will accept you.

One of the things that makes successful people different from unsuccessful people is their mentality about themselves. Successful people believe in themselves while unsuccessful people doubt themselves. Many people do not believe in themselves because of what they have gone through, because of negative things which people have said to them, and because of their socio-economic background. They have limited themselves to the status quo because of how they view themselves. How do you see yourself? Do you believe in yourself? Many people have placed limitations on themselves as to how far they will go in life. The power of "I" is no more in them. They now think in collective terms, rather than individual terms. They don't see themselves making it ALONE, but rather with THEM.

It is a pity that many people have allowed their social, spiritual, physical, cultural and psychological background and situations to kill their God given "ego" or the "I" which is in them. Remember this, if no one believes in you, God believes in you. Why? It is because what He said about you in Jeremiah 29:11: *"For I know the plans I have for you,"* declares the Lord, *"plans to prosper you and not to harm you, plans to give you hope and a future."* The original plan of God for everyone is to prosper or to succeed. The gene for success is inherent in everybody. God is a successful being, and He has created us to be successful because His DNA is in us. That is why God is always looking for people who believe in themselves and who will manifest His Omnipotency that is in them. God's potency and potential for success is in us. That is why you need to believe in yourself and not in what someone says about you. The following heroes in the Bible who were successful in every facet of their lives demonstrated this great faith and belief in themselves.

- ❖ Isaiah believed in himself and said to God, "Here I am, send me."
- ❖ David believed in himself and said, "I will not die but live."
- ❖ Paul believed in himself and said, "I press on…"
- ❖ Ruth the Moabitess believed in herself and said, "Where you go I will go, and where you stay I will stay."
- ❖ Jacob believed in himself and said, "I will not leave you except you bless me."

Everything in life depends on how you see yourself and the "I" that is in you. This self-confidence always brings courage, determination, perseverance, and endurance. What are you doing with yourself? You will remain disabled and immobile in life if you allow self-pity, inferiority complex, and persecution complex to dominate your life. Believe in yourself even if nobody does…

Believe in Your Ability

"I can"

The English word "can" is an auxiliary verb (a helping verb). It is different from the word "may." The word "can" indicates ability whereas "may" indicates possibility. The word "can" here shows that there is ability in you. The fact remains that there is ability and capability in everyone. There is something which you are made for. There is something which you can do. There is something inside you. You are like a container that contains something. The problem is that many people never discover themselves as well as their abilities. They don't know what they are made for or manufactured to be in life. They idolize the abilities of other people while they devalue and disbelieve their own.

Apostle Paul here recognizes that there is a God's given ability for enablement to succeed in life in him. God created and designed every one of us uniquely with certain abilities and potentialities to succeed in life. Therefore, as you believe in yourself, you also need to believe in your ability, that is, what God has created you for in life. There is a "can" in you. Or let me say, God has "canned" [created] you for something. You are like a can or a bottle of Coke. You are not empty. There is something in you. There is ability in you. There is potentiality in you. There is something in you that will give way to success. You must know it and believe it.

If you don't discover yourself you will remain covered in life.

When you know and believe what you are "canned" [created] for in life, then the word "can't" will be removed from your vocabulary. What are you "canned" [created] to be in life? You need to discover it, believe it, and pursuit it. But you must believe that you can be whatever God wants you to be in life. Do not limit yourself to what people want you to be. You have more capacity and capability than you think you are. God has created you with enough space and capacity in your hard drive for your maximum output of success in life. God has wired you for something. There is something inside you that is useful and needed in your generation. You are created to be a reason to a season, a solution to a situation, and an answer to a question. You are not just a statistics for success, but a maker of success. There is success in you. You are "canned" [created] for success. But you need to know and believe in what you are "canned" [created] for...

❖ Abraham knew and believed what he was meant to be in life – Father of all nations.
❖ Jacob knew and believed what he was meant to be in life – Israel.

❖ Joseph knew and believed what he was meant to be in life – Provider for his family.

❖ Moses knew and believed what he was meant to be in life – Great deliverer.

❖ John the Baptist knew and believed what he was meant to be in life – Forerunner of Jesus.

❖ Jesus Christ knew and believed what He was meant to be in life – Savior of the world.

Remember this: you can never be fulfilled and satisfied in any area of life in which God has not "canned" [created] you for. Life and living in the area where you are not "canned" [created] will lead to a life of probability instead of ability; struggle instead of success; survival instead of accomplishment; breakdown instead of breakthrough; endurance instead of enjoyment; and I can't instead of I can. What are you "canned" [created] for in life?

Believe in Your Efforts

"I can do"

The word "do" here is a word of action and effort. Paul did not say, "I can wish all things". No. But I can do. What a practical and realistic statement! God will only enable you to make it and succeed in life if you are willing to motivate yourself by putting more efforts and not just wishing.

Many people settle for wishing in life and never get to the level of doing. It is good to desire, but it is best to do. Desire cannot become acquire unless you perspire. You have to add efforts to your dreams. Dreaming without doing will lead to daydreaming. Successful people are not just dreamers but are great doers. There is one thing to know what God "canned" [created] you for in life; there is another thing to make it happen. Life is not just about incubation, nursing an idea, but about manifestation, realizing the idea. No wonder someone says that an idea is like wheelbarrow, unless you push it, it will remain there. You have to do something if you want something to happen in your life.

You must be willing to pursue whatever you believe you are canned and created for in life. Stop praying about it; pursue it. For how long have you been wishing and contemplating? Stop it. Inspiration without action will lead to illusion. Motivation without action will lead to delusion. Faith without action will lead to failure. Faith with action will lead to success. Therefore, you need to take actions that will lead to your success because...

Unless you do it you cannot become it.

Let us take a cue from the yearly Grammy and Oscar awards. The awards for success are only for actors and actresses who have done something and they are never given to spectators. There is no Best Film Watcher Award. Unfortunately, there is no award for anyone who has watched the highest number of movies. But there are awards for those who have made best movies. Do you see the revelation? The world rewards doers and not non-doers. Therefore, God did not create anyone to be a spectator in life, but rather to be a doer and achiever. You can never achieve in life if you don't do something. Hear what the Bible says in the following passages:

Deut. 28:12

*"The LORD will open the heavens, the storehouse of his bounty, to send rain on your land in season and to **bless all the work of your hands**. You will lend to many nations but will borrow from none."*

Proverbs 14:23

"All hard work brings a profit, but mere talk leads only to poverty." (NIV)

"Hard work always pays off; mere talk puts no bread on the table." (Message)

"Work brings profit, but mere talk leads to poverty." (Contemporary Bible)

Hard work here does not suggest over activity, over work and over struggle, but skillfulness and diligence.

Proverbs 12:24

"Diligent hands will rule, but laziness ends in slave labor."

Prov. 22:29

"Do you see a man skilled in his work? He will serve before kings; he will not serve before obscure men." (NIV)

"Observe people who are good at their work— skilled workers are always in demand and admired; they don't take a backseat to anyone." (The Message)

"If you do your job well, you will work for a ruler and never be a slave." (Contemporary Bible)

Ecclesiastes 10:10

"Remember: The duller the ax the harder the work; Use your head: The more brains, the less muscle." (The Message)

In whatever you do in life, you need to motivate yourself by seeking to be the best and being professional. Update yourself so that you will not become outdated.

Believe in Your Scope

"I can do all things"

Again, Apostle Paul describes the spheres, domain, scope, and the areas in which God will give him enablement to succeed in life: **ALL THINGS**. The word translated *"all things"* from Greek means any, every, whatsoever, and everything.

Here Paul refuses to put any unnecessary limitations and barriers on himself. Therefore, according to him, there is no limit to what you can become in life. Do not allow anything to limit you and what you can become in life. There is no limit to what anyone can become in life. The only limit is the one which you set for yourself. You cannot go beyond the limit of the limitation which you have set for yourself. There is no limit to where you can go in life.

God who created you is unlimited in His resources and His scope. With Him all things are possible. Not just a few things, but all things. You have to believe in the scope of "all things" as against "few things." You have to develop the mentality of "all things." You have to think beyond the level of "few things." Remember that as a man thinks, so he is. Therefore...

- ❖ Do not complain about your age. Abraham was 75 when God called him and 100 when he gave birth to Isaac. Caleb also was 86 when he requested for and fought for his inheritance.
- ❖ Do not complain about your lack of education. Peter had no education, but allowed himself to be taught by Jesus.

❖ Do not complain about your past mistakes and background. Remember Rahab the harlot, Ruth, Esther, Daniel, and Paul. They all had bad pasts.

❖ Do not complain that you don't have parents. Esther did not but she became a queen.

Let me tell you this: even if you cannot do special and extraordinary things in life, you can still do "greater things." Believe in your scope...

Believe in your Source

"I can do all things through Christ"

The Amplified Bible gives a wonderful translation of this part based on the Greek translation: *"I have strength for all things in Christ Who empowers me."* What a brilliant translation. Here, the Bible is saying that you must believe in the source of your power for success. You are not the source of your power for success. It is not your degree; it is not your smartness; it is not your skillfulness; it is not how many people that you know; and in fact it is not your background. The source of your success is Jesus Christ.

UNLESS HE IS YOUR SOURCE, HE CANNOT BE YOUR RESOURCE

Success is not to believe in yourself alone; it is also to believe in your source. Your source is your foundation. Your source is your origin. Your source is your root. You cannot do anything without knowing your source. You must believe in your source. You are the outcome of your source. Your source is the key to your resources. Jesus Christ is your source. He is the source of your power for success. He is the source of your key to success. He is the secret behind your success.

Jesus Christ suffered, died on the cross, and redeemed you so that you will not be a failure in life. Because He did not fail, then you must not. Because He accomplished a lot, then you must. You have to believe in your source of success, that which is Jesus. Without Him, there is nothing you can become. Believing in Him is not a catalyst for failure. My brethren, I want you to know that spirituality is never a criterion for failure, but rather for success. If truly Christ is in you then you are destined for, *"the hope of glory"* (Col. 1:27). It is now time for you to realize the dynamic of your source and stop having defeat in mentality, poverty mentality, struggle mentality, suffering mentality, and warfare mentality. Rather, you must believe in your source and begin to have overcoming mentality, success mentality, progress mentality, and accomplishment mentality.

Believe in your Power

"I can do all things through Christ who strengthens me"

You must believe in the power of your source. Your source is not a docile, inactive, and passive source. Rather, it is a powerful source. It is a dynamic source. It is an active source. It is a source that can empower, strengthen, and enable you for success. In other words, if you have accepted Jesus into your life and if He is living in you, then you carry the highest voltage in you. You carry the voltage of the Holy Spirit for success, promotion, accomplishment and achievement.

Do you notice that the word "strengthens" in this verse is a present continuous tense? This means, the source of power for success is always on and abiding in you. No wonder He said in Philippians 1:6 that, *"Being confident of this, that he who began a good work in you will carry it on to completion until the day of Christ Jesus."* That is why you cannot quit because of failure. That is why you cannot give up because of setback. There is a power of continuity and resiliency in you. You have to activate it to work for you.

The Amplified Bible translates this power as *"inner strength."* It is something that is working inside you to produce the outside success in your life. In other words, the power of your success is from the inside and not from the outside. It is He that is in you that will make you the WHO that you will become. For Daniel, this inner power is called "an excellent Spirit." (Dan. 6:3) For Joseph, it is called, "the LORD was with." (Gen. 39:2) For Nehemiah, it is called, "the gracious hand of God." (Nehemiah 2:8) For Paul, it is called, "the grace of God." Hear what Paul says about this power in Ephesians 3:20: *"Now to him who is able to do immeasurably more than all we ask or imagine, according to his **power** that is at work within us"* (NIV). The Amplified Bible renders it this way: *"Now to Him Who, by (in consequence of) the [action of His] power that is at work within us, is able to [carry out His purpose and] do superabundantly, far over and above all that we [dare] ask or think [infinitely beyond our highest prayers, desires, thoughts, hopes, or dreams]."*

You can succeed in life. Success is not only for the unbelievers. It is not for certain people. It is for believers or Christians as well. However, success does not just come by wishing or daydreaming. You have to motivate yourself intrinsically (internally), extrinsically (externally), spiritually, and physically.

CHAPTER FOUR

Move Yourself From Complacence to Excellence

> *"Responsibility is the key to possibility while irresponsibility is the gateway to impossibility."*

Complacence is one of the major self-made diseases that cause stagnancy in life. Complacence has been defined as calm or secure satisfaction with oneself. It is a feeling of quiet pleasure or security, self-satisfaction or smug satisfaction with an existing situation. Complacency is different from contentment.

Contentment is acknowledgement and satisfaction of reaching capacity. It is a state of mind whereby one's desires are confined to his lot in whatever it may be (1 Tim. 6:6; 2 Cor. 9:8). It is to accept the reality of your situation without complaint or resentment. When you are content you work on those things that you can change and accept those you cannot and you will refuse to be disheartened. On the other hand, when you are complacent, you will adopt a mentality of "I am good enough" or "I am alright now." You become satisfied with mediocrity, with no real aspirations to do and be more.

Complacency is the feeling you have when you are satisfied with yourself. A complacent person doesn't bother again to strive for dreams because he or she is happy the way he or she is. A content person, on the other hand, knows that God has called them to something bigger than the current situation.

Complacent people always complain silently or loudly, secretly or publicly. They don't aim high, they don't dream high, and they are afraid of trying...They can talk, but cannot do. They procrastinate and postpone... They are always waiting for the right time and season before they will do...and will not do anything. Excellent people, on the other hand don't settle for the less. They may be contented and grateful for what God has done for them, but they still expect more... They believe that they can be better...

Excellence is being better. It is achieving or accomplishing more. It is to excel in what you do. It is a state of being the best, being distinguished, being above, being exceptional, being in good standing, and being above the past. In 1 Peter 2:9 we are described in the following ways: *"But you are a chosen race, a royal priesthood, a dedicated nation, [God's] own purchased, special people, that you may set forth the wonderful deeds and display the virtues and perfections of Him Who called you out of darkness into His marvelous light."* [Amplified] The Lord has saved us so that we can *"display the virtues and perfections of Him."* That is to say, to display His excellence. Don't forget that He is an excellent God. Therefore, becoming excellent in life is possible. Then, how can you move from complacence to excellence based on Matthew 14:28-33?

Resilience

"And Peter answered Him, 'Lord, if it is You, command
me to come to You on the water' " [v. 28]

The disciples along with Peter were going through a serious storm and crisis. Jesus had commanded them to go to the other side and they were journeying to this other side. Verse 24 of Matthew 14 says that when they were in the middle of the sea or the journey, there arose a serious storm and wind against their boat. The boat was their safety nest and their comfort zone. The boat was what their only means of crossing to the other side. They were very used to the boat. The boat was used for their fishing business and now for transportation. They have tied their lives around the boat. But there was a storm and wind rising against the boat.

What is your own boat? Your boat may be your job, your business, your degree, your diploma, your certificate, your license, your relationship and so on. Your boat is what you use as a means of survival. Your boat is what gives you comfort, security, safety, meaning, and purpose in life. Your boat is what defines and describes your life.

Sometimes the Lord will rock your boat so that He can take you to the other side. The Lord will allow wind to rock your boat, so that He can move you to excellence.

While the other disciples who were in the boat were struggling to save the boat and their lives, Peter took another route. Instead of resistance and rescue attitude, Peter developed what is called resilience. Resilience is that ineffable quality that allows some people to be knocked down by life and come back stronger than ever. Resilience is refusing to give up even if wind or storm has hit the boat. While others in the boat were crying, complaining, nagging, and blaming Jesus when they saw Him walking toward them in the boat, Peter made this resilient statement, *"Lord, if it is You, command me to come to You on the water."*

Peter said, Lord, I am tired of staying in this boat. I have been known with this boat. I am tired of where I am; I want to be where you are. Who are you looking up to?

To reach excellence in life, you must focus on excellence. You must not go down with your boat. You must bounce back. This is the problem with complacent guys; they go down with the boat of their lives. But Peter said, I am not ready to stay in this boat again; I can go to an excellent level. I also can walk on the water... At least my Master is walking on the water. Who do you make as the model or focus of your life? You must have one. You must have someone that will provoke you, challenge you, motivate you, and inspire you when you are about to give up...You must be resilient if you want to be excellent in life.

To be resilient means that you refuse to be defeated. You refuse to sink with the boat. You will refuse to give up trying. You divert your energy from going down to staying on the water, from mourning your failure or loss to improving yourself. Resilience means that you don't allow your failure to become your undertaker, but rather your caretaker. Resilience means that you are willing and ready to do something different when something is not going on well. Resilience is *believing* in God to open another door when one door has been closed in your life. It is being tough when things go tough. You have to be resilient if you want to excel and succeed in life.

Reposition

"He said, 'Come!' So Peter got out of the boat..." [v. 29a]

The Master of the universe as well as water told Peter to come. Peter asked for permission to change his location and position. It was not a geographical or spatial location, but a psychological location. Sometimes, the key to excellence is not about geographical relocation, but psychological relocation. He had been living and staying with boat lovers, boat loafers, complacent people, and people with mediocrity. But he decided to relocate, reposition, and change his mind about his location. Sometimes you have to change your mind about where you are if you want to get there. You have to make up your mind to change your location. Therefore, because Peter was willing to change his position, the Lord told him to come. The Lord is always willing to help you if you are willing to make a change. What did Peter do when the Lord told him to come? The Bible says, *"So Peter got out of the boat."*

Peter had to get out of the boat if he were to become excellent in life. Like the other disciples, so many people have developed addiction towards their boat. They have become addicted to certain things, situations, habits, and conditions in their lives. The problem is not that they cannot get out of it, but they have not decided to get out of it. They are not willing to break away from what has been holding them back from God and from progressing in life. Yours may be a habit, a relationship, a way of life, a friendship, a situation, a condition, and so on. You must break the addiction to that boat that has held you down and back in life. Your addiction will limit your distinction. Sometimes where you position yourself will determine how far you will be and how far you will go in life. Sometimes your position will determine your promotion. Your position will determine your disposition. Your position will determine your condition. How have you positioned yourself?

Do you know that you can be addicted to the position and condition you are in life that you don't even bother to better yourself? For how long will you continue to receive that same amount which you are receiving for the past years? The Bible says that, *"So Peter got out of the boat..."* You have to rise up and get out of the boat of that income which you are making. You have to rise up and get of the boat of that sameness you are in life. You are more than that boat. You are bigger and better than that boat.

What are you addicted to that has made you complacent and mediocre in life? You have been in that boat for long... You need to get out. Listen to this, *Doing the same thing in life will bring you the same result in life.*

The boat may look good and nice now, but it will sink if you don't get out of it. Listen to this: Peter did not bother if Andrew, John, James or any one of them would want to get out of the boat. Sometimes you have to do it alone. They may be okay with the boat, but Peter decided to get out of it. Sometimes you have to leave some friends or some people behind if you desire to excel in life. You have to get out even if others are afraid to get out... If you don't leave that place you cannot get to that place... If you don't leave them you cannot be ahead of them.

You have to step out of the boat of limitation, fear, low self-esteem, procrastination, complaints, anger, seeking acceptance, uncertainty, contemplation, blaming, addiction, excuses... Always remember that, *whatever you don't put behind will put you behind in life.*

Risk

"....and walked on the water, and he came toward Jesus." [v. 29b]

Peter did not only reposition himself, he also took a risk. Peter did what was unthinkable, unimaginable, and unexplainable. He began to walk on the water toward Jesus. He took a risk. Here is the truth: If you do not take a risk in life you will be at risk in life.

To take a risk is to do what others are not ready to do or what others have never done before. It is to do the unusual. It is to do the unimaginable. It is to go the extra mile. It has been proven that those who do what others have never done before always experienced results which others have never experienced before.

49

If you want to be different in life, do something different. Peter did something different. He took a risk and walked on the water. Walked on the water? Yes... No one has ever done that before..., but Peter did it.

Peter did the unusual. He did not attempt to swim in the water, the normal thing to do, but he decided to walk on water, the abnormal thing to do. If you expect an unusual result, you must take unusual steps. You must be ready to take a risk. Taking a risk is to try or make an effort. The major failure in life is failure to take a risk. Many people are afraid to take a risk because they don't want to fail. It is better to try and fail than to fail to try. Fear of failure is the key to failure and failure to try is trying to fail.

If you want to experience the unusual in your life, begin to do the unusual. Queen Esther risked her life to do what was not expected of her to do. She even said before she did it that: "If I die, I die." She was ready to die while trying. But she did not die. What usually kills dreams, goals, visions, and excellence in life is not willing to try and not willing to take a risk.

Peter said that if walking on the water would make him different and give him excellence, then he would take the risk. Why can't you take that risk that would make you become excellent in life? Why can't you go back to school? Why can't you go for that degree program? Why can't you go for that Master's degree program? Why can't you go further? Why can't you invest in that business? Why can't you take that job? Why can't you commit into that relationship? Why can't you make that proposal to marry that man or woman? Why can't you answer the call of God to go into the ministry? Why can't you settle down with that woman or man in marriage? Why can't you...? Maybe your answer is this: "I am afraid." Yes, it is normal to be afraid, but you are to take the risk. You can never know that you can do it unless you take the risk. You can never know that you can make it unless you take a risk. You can never know that God will help you, unless you take a risk.

Many people have been contemplating on walking on their water all this while, but they are afraid and still waiting for when the water will subside. They are waiting for when condition will be alright before they will go back to school, enroll in the class, begin the project, begin that thing, stop that habit, learn about that computer, invest in that business, and so on. Hear what Solomon says in Ecclesiastes 11:4-6:

> [4] *"He who observes the wind [and waits for all conditions to be favorable] will not sow, and he who regards the clouds will not reap.* [5] *As you know not what is the way of the wind, or how the spirit comes to the bones in the womb of a pregnant woman, even so you know not the work of God, Who does all.* [6] *In the morning sow your seed, and in the evening withhold not your hands, for you know not which shall prosper, whether this or that, or whether both alike will be good."* [Amplified]

Another risk which Peter took was that he came toward Jesus. This is the same Jesus whom many of them thought to be a ghost. He came toward Jesus who told him to come. He has a focus. His risk was based on focus. That is, he knew what he was risking his life for. He was not playing games or gambling with his life. He had a focus - going toward Jesus who told him to come. He did not deviate from his focus. Jesus was his focus. He decided to get to his focus. What is your focus and what are you doing to get to it? Where are you heading to? Life without destination is a waste. Or let me ask you again, who told you to do what you are doing? Who told you to go to where you are going? Are you acting on God's will or on your own will? Are you acting on revelation or on information? Peter responded to revelation and not information. My prayer to you is that God will give you revelation that will lead to your excellence and distinction...

However, the problem with many people is that they want to come to Him (Jesus) or to their purpose, but they still want to be in the boat. They want to move ahead and still want to stay behind. They want to come to Jesus, but still want to hang out with them in boat. They want a leg outside the boat and a leg inside the boat. They have not made up their minds... They have not taken the risk... If you want to become excellent in your spiritual life and walk with Jesus, you must come to Him on the water... If you want to become excellent in your career, relationship, education, and so on, you must take the risk of getting out of the boat and move toward your goal.

Request

"But when he perceived and felt the strong wind,
he was frightened, and as he began to sink, he cried
out, 'Lord, save me' [from death]!" [v. 30]

Thank God for Peter. Thank God for trying. Thank God for taking steps toward excellence. But the unexpected happened to Peter. That is what usually happens when you take risks. The unexpected always happens. Sometimes you win, sometimes you lose. Sometimes it works; sometimes it does not work. The Bible says in verse 30 that Peter perceived and felt the strong wind and was afraid. The NIV says, *"But when he saw the wind, he was afraid."*

Remember that the wind had always been there. It was the wind that was hitting their boat. It was on top of the wind and water that he saw Jesus walking on the water. It was in the midst of the wind that he asked Peter to come to Him on the water. It was in the midst of the wind that Peter stepped out of the boat. The wind was there. The wind will not go because you are doing the will of God. The wind will not go because you obey the Lord. The wind will not go because He tells you to come. The wind will not go because you have taken risks. Sometimes what you are running away from will not run away from you.

Your wind may be disappointment. Your wind may be failure. Your wind may be sickness. Your wind may be divorce. Your wind may be your limitation. Your wind may be harassment. Your wind may be bullying. Your wind may be fear. Your wind may be what you are going through now. Your wind may be spiritual attack. Everybody has a wind. You cannot run away from your wind. You have to face and deal with your wind. The Bible says that Peter was afraid. The New Living Translation says, *"He was terrified."* The Message Bible says, *"He lost his nerve."* He lost his courage. He lost the courage to continue… He wanted to go back to the boat.

Sometimes the wind will make you think you have taken the wrong step. Sometimes the wind will make you regret your actions. Sometimes the wind will make you accuse God. The purpose of the wind is to change your focus, to change your goal, to distract you from your goal, and to make you see your limitations. Your wind is to pull you down…

What happened when Peter saw the wind? The Bible describes it in three words: "Beginning to sink." That is, he began to sink. He had no lifeboat around. He had no life jacket on himself. He had no safety device. He was on the sea. He began to sink. Despite the fact that you are doing what God wants you to do does not mean that you cannot sink. Sometimes God will let you go down before He will let you go up. Don't be afraid of sinking. *The Lord will let you sink before He will make you soar. The Lord will let you breakdown before you can breakthrough.* Sometimes you have to go through the water or fire so that you can come out excellent.

Don't blame and criticize Peter for sinking. At least he tried and attempted to do something that was different. Anybody can be in the boat doing nothing. Anybody can be in the boat watching and praying. Anybody can be in the boat crying and whining. But it takes a person with courage, faith, determination, and commitment to step out of the boat and walk on water.

But what do you do when you are going down? What do you do when you are down? What did Peter do? The Bible says that, *"He cried out, Lord, save me."* This is not the time to blame and complain; it is the time to ask for help. It is the time to request. It is the time to reach out and ask for help.

The problem is that many people fail to ask or request for help when they are sinking in their problems. They put on good masks to cover their problems. They are too holy and too strong to request for help. They don't ask God for help in prayers and don't ask people who can be of help to them. They don't seek for spiritual, nor for professional help as well. Instead, they are seeking for supernatural or mystical help. They are looking for magic. Sometimes they think they are supermen or superwomen. They act as if they don't have problems or have never had problems. But Peter did not. Instead, he cried to Jesus for help.

Complacency will not make you ask for help. Complacency will make you think that you have all the answers. Complacency will not make you listen to the advice of others. Being a fisherman before, Peter did not say that he knew how to swim. He asked for help. You cannot know how to do everything. There is something that you don't know how to do. Do you seek for help? Do you seek for the help of God? Do you seek for the help of professionals? Don't just pray about your condition; ask for help. In the Bible:

- Joseph asked for the help of the butler and the baker.
- Mordecai asked for the help of Esther.
- Nehemiah asked for the help of the King.
- Jehoshaphat asked for the help of God.

God is able to bring you out of your miry place to solid ground only if you ask for His help. Here is another revelation: Peter did not ask for help from those who were in the boat... What help can someone who is a mediocre and who does not desire excellence in life give you? What advice would someone who has no purpose and dreams in life give you? You will only end up like them. Peter decided to ask for the help of someone who has walked on this water...and who is still walking on the water... The Lord of the water. Who do you cry to when you are sinking?

Resources

"Instantly Jesus reached out His hand and caught and held him, saying to him, 'O you of little faith, why did you doubt.' " [v.31]

To become excellent in life you will need resources. A resource has been defined as, "a source of supply, support, or aid, especially one that can be readily drawn upon when needed." It is what you will fall upon when you need help. It is the support and aid that is available when you are sinking or failing. You will need hands that will pull you up.

When Peter cried for help, the Lord Jesus reached His hand to him. Thank God for the availability of the hand of Jesus that pulled Peter up. The hand that can never fail. The hand that is reliable. The hand that is stronger than any other hands. The hand that will never let you down. The everlasting hand. The eternal hand. The omnipotent hand. The hand of the Lord...

The hand of the Lord can reach you wherever you are and pull you out of your wherever situation you find yourself. But can the hand of the Lord reach you? The only thing that can shorten and block the hands of God in your life is sin. Hear what Isaiah 59:1-2 says: *"Behold, the Lord's hand is not shortened at all, that it cannot save, nor His ear dull with deafness, that it cannot hear. But your iniquities have made a separation between you and your God, and your sins have hidden His face from you, so that He will not hear."* [Amplified].

Like Peter, you need someone who is up there and who is not sinking to lift or pull you up. You need someone who will hold you by the hand and pull you up. Unfortunately, many people are surrounded, without knowing, with people who are pulling them down. People who will add to their problems. People who will discourage them. People who will doubt them. People who do not believe in them. People who condemn them. People who criticize them. They may be their spouses, friends, relatives, siblings, colleagues, co-workers, parents, family members, church members, and so on. But here are the questions: How many people have you pulled down or how many people have you pulled up?

Many people rely on hands that will fail them. Many people rely on hands that cannot hold them. Many people rely on the hands of the flesh. Many people rely on the hands that will pull them down. You need the hand of God and you also need the hands of reliable and godly people to pull you up when you are sinking or down. You need lifters and not doubters, discouragers, killers, deceivers, takers, manipulators, and so on.

You need the following hands of resources in your life if you want to become excellent in life:

- The Spiritual Hand (the hand of God) e.g. Peter and Jesus Christ
- The Relational Hand (Connection with People) e.g. Esther
- The Positional Hand (hand of someone higher than you) e.g. Joseph and Nehemiah
- The Educational Hand (Knowledge) e.g. Daniel
- The Technological Hand (Information)

What kind of resources are you using to get to where you are going in life? Is it cheating, bad association, lying, fraud, selling your body, evil powers, voodoos, and so on. Remember this: If God is not the source of it, He will not resource it.

But wait a minute! Peter reached out to the Lord before the Lord reached out to Him. He did not just stay there doing nothing. The Lord held him by the hand because his (Peter's) hand was stretched out to the Lord. If you want the Lord to hold you, you must hold on to the Lord. But here is another problem, many people are not looking for help or for helpers, but they are looking for who will carry them or who will carry their burdens. They are looking for someone who would do everything for them while they will not lift any fingers. Jesus did not jump into the water and become wet so that He could help Peter. Here comes the truth: *"Don't let people pull you into their storms... Instead pull them into your peace."* Do not become a burden to people in the name of helping you, and don't become entrapped in people's problems in the name of helping them.

Jesus reached out His hand to Peter to lift him up. Jesus gave him a hope and encouragement. Jesus held his hand and told him, "Peter, you can make it." The Lord is telling someone or you today that you can make it. You may have been at the point of giving up, sinking, going down, and quitting, but the Lord is saying to you as He said to Peter that, "You can make it." He is saying again that, "What you need is to lean on me and let me hold you." You cannot hold yourself. You cannot do it by yourself. You need the hand of Jesus... You need the hands of good friends... You need the hands of godly people... You need good hands.

Maybe you have been trying all this while to walk on the water, to stay above those circumstances in your life, to move on toward your destination in life, to better your life, and to become excellent in life, but it seems you are sinking. It seems that the more you try, the more you sink. God will help you up. Always remember that you can excel in life.

CHAPTER FIVE

Know What to Do When You Don't Know What to Do

> *"God will use what is available for you to provide what is not available for you."*

L ife is always full of unexpected expectations. Sometimes what you expect is not what you experience; and what you experience is not what you expect. Life is full of surprises. Some are ugly while some are good. Sometimes things are not as we expect them to be. Situations in life are unpredictable. They can change to the worst and they can change to the best. That is why we say life is not fair. Unfair situations always come without announcing them. They come anytime, at any stage of life. But what do you do when life becomes unfair to you?

The situation at hand was a wedding ceremony. This is always an elaborate social ceremony in Israel. It is a communal event. It always brings the whole community and family together. It always ends with 7 days of marriage parties at the house of the groom's father. And serving of wine is the major thing in this party. Therefore, shortage of wine would be a disgrace to the groom's father and entire family. Since wine signifies happiness and merriment, then what happens when your wine is no more? What happens when your joy is taken away? What happens when those things that are making you happy are no more? Verse 3 of the passage tells us the cause and the source of the problem. The New Living Translation says, *"The wine supply ran out during the festivities."* The New King James Version says, *"And when they ran out of wine."* What happens when you run out of peace, joy, happiness, finances, and so on? That you have run out does not mean it is over. Someone said, *"Everything will be okay in the end. If it is not okay, then it is not the end"*. The groom as well as the father of the groom did not know what to do when wine was gone. Therefore, what do you do when you don't know what to do? You will need to do the followings as found in John 2:1-11.

Invitation

"And Jesus and his disciples had also been invited to the wedding." [v. 2]

The celebrants did not make the mistake of inviting other guests and not inviting Jesus Christ, the Greatest Guest. What does this mean? This means that sometimes many people only invite Jesus Christ into their problems and not into their lives as their Lord and personal savior. Therefore, inviting Jesus is more than coming to the church. It is not praying to Him to solve your problem. It is more than believing in Him or knowing Him. It is to have Him living and dwelling in you.

The problem with many people is that they only invite Jesus after the wine is gone. That is, they only invite Him into their lives after certain problems have befallen them. But the bride and bridegroom for this wedding did not make that mistake. They did not put the cart before the horse. They did not invite Jesus after the wine has gone. They were very smart. They had already invited Him. Jesus was already in the house before the problem came. Jesus was already around before the problem came. But it does not matter when you invite Him. He is always available to come if you invite Him. Have you invited Him when you don't know what to do?

Jesus is the best friend you can even have and which many have not had. Other friends and guests would leave, desert, and abandon you when things go wrong with you. Before you know it, you are left on your own. But Jesus will never leave you. Hear what He said in Hebrews 13:5-6: *"Keep your lives free from the love of money and be content with what you have, because God has said, 'Never will I leave you; never will I forsake you.' So we say with confidence, 'The Lord is my helper; I will not be afraid. What can mere mortals do to me?'*

I don't know any words of assurance that are better and greater than this. Nobody can give you such words assurance except Jesus.

When was the last time that you invited Him into your life? When was the last time you invited Him into that situation in your life? When was the last time you invited Him when you didn't know what to do?

You may be at that point in your life when you don't know what to do. Maybe your marriage or relationship is falling apart; your home is on fire; you have just been fired at work; you want to make a decision about your life or something has just gone wrong in your life, and so on. Maybe you are asking yourself, what can I do? You need to invite Jesus. Just try Him and you will never be ashamed. Jesus is not only Lord of your salvation, He is also Lord of your situations.

Information

*"When the wine was gone, Jesus' mother said to
him, "They have no more wine." [v. 3]*

Jesus was not just there as a figurehead. He was different from other guests at the occasion. Mary, His mother, recognized this fact. She knew that even though He had never performed any miracle, yet, He is still the Lord of lords and the King of kings.

You must know that if Jesus is in your life, He can also be in charge of your problems and worries only if you keep Him informed. Sometimes, we only reduce Christ to the inside and we think that He cannot handle what is happening in our outside. He is both Lord of the inside and Lord of the outside. If He can or has saved you from sin, He can also save you from any problems that you are facing. The only condition for His intervention is informing Him. That is, you have to tell Him. You have to speak to Him. It is not about crying, complaining, whining, being angry at God and everybody, or hating God and everybody. It is about praying to Him.

Mary was not ready to lose her mind over what she could not handle. Therefore, when others were getting worried and upset, Mary went and informed Jesus. No one was willing to help. No one could offer any solution and suggestion. Sometimes that situation will come in your life when those around you cannot offer any solutions to your problem. That is when you need to speak to Jesus. Did anybody know that Jesus was there? Did anybody know that He could do something? Did anybody know that with God all things are possible? I think only Mary did. When others limited what He can do, Mary did not.

Where were the other guests? What were they doing? Just wait until your wine is gone then you will know the kinds of friends you have. Some will desert you. Some will mock you.

Some will laugh at you. Some will talk about you. Some will gossip about you

Let me tell you this, you will have to let go of some guests in your life if you want to experience greater manifestation in your life. Some relationships have to go. Some friends have to go. Some things have to go. They have to give way for Jesus to intervene in your life…

But I love what Mary did; she informed Him and left.

Who do you inform when your wine is gone? When things go bad and tough, who do you inform? Some people inform the wrong people. Some people inform their friends. Some people inform their relatives. Some people inform their colleagues. Some people inform their therapists. Some people inform their attorneys. Some people inform their physicians. Some people inform their spouses. Some people inform…

No one cares to inform Jesus. Only few care to inform Jesus. People only inform Jesus when all the people they have informed have failed them. You have to know that only Christ can offer you the best and final solutions. Others can try, but they cannot provide a lasting solution. If God cannot do it, NO ONE can do it for you…

Inclusion

"Woman, why do you involve me?" Jesus replied.
"My hour has not yet come." [v. 4]

Here are the questions: Did you include Christ in that decision that you made or that you are making? Did you involve Christ before you took that step? Did you involve Christ in those things that you are doing? Listen to this: If He does not begin it, He cannot complete it.

When things get out of hand, people usually take steps or do things they feel are the best solutions. Sometimes, those things will add more to the problems. There is nothing wrong in involving people to help you in what you are going through, but learn to involve God first. Unless you involve Him, He will not solve it. Remember that...

- The widow who was the wife of one of the prophets involved God through Elisha when she was faced with the problem of debt in 2 Kings 4:1-7.
- The sons of the prophet involved Elisha when the axe head which one of them was using fell into the river in 2 kings 6:1-7.
- Mary and Martha involved Jesus when their brother, Lazarus, died in John 11.
- The disciples of Jesus involved Him when storms and winds rose against their boat in Mark 4:35-41.

Mary did not involve the wrong people as some do, but she involved the right Master. She did not go to the father or parents of the groom. She did not go to the friends of the groom. She did not go to the chairman and chairlady of the occasion. She did not go to the Master of the ceremony of the day. She did not go to the head of the cook. Instead, she went to involve the Lord of all situations.

However, when you involve Him, you must wait for His time. Involving Him does not mean rushing Him. It must be at His own time. That is why many people do not want to involve Him. They think He is too slow to act. They want a quick fix to their problem. They want a drive-through kind of solution, but Jesus does not offer that. You must be ready and willing to wait for His time if you expect any solution and intervention from Him. It cannot be at your dictate. It cannot be at your pace. It cannot be on your term. It must be at His. Hear what Paul said in Romans 8:19,

"For the creation waits in eager expectation for the children of God to be revealed." There must be waiting before there will be revealing. There must be expectation before there will be manifestation. There are many who are in their waiting period. I want to tell you today that your solution is on the way... Just wait for His time. Don't rush Him. Don't rush it. Don't rush your solution. It is not how soon, but how well.

Impression

"His mother said to the servants, 'Do whatever he tells you.' "[v. 5]

Another way out to what you can do when you don't know what to do is to do whatever He tells you to do. Can you do it? You must be ready to obey Him. You must be ready to do things in His own way and not in your own way. Sometimes His way may be crude, obsolete, unconventional, outdated, unpopular, unscientific, unorthodox, unconservative, and unphilosophical; it is the best way. How do you solve your problem? Some people do what they are told to do. Some people do what their minds tell them to do. Some people do not know what to do and do not do anything. Some people are still praying...

Mary knew that Jesus believed in doing. She knew that nothing will just happen unless something is done. What are you doing... to solve your problem...?

This point says you have to impress Jesus. To impress, means to do something that will please somebody. This is called obedience. Are you doing what you are doing to impress someone or to impress yourself? Do you impress God? In other words, is God happy with what you are doing?

John Sammis, the writer of the popular Hymn "Trust and Obey," said:

> *When we walk with the Lord in the light of His Word,*
> *What a glory He sheds on our way!*
> *While we do His good will, He abides with us still,*
> *And with all who will trust and obey.*
> *Chorus*
> *Trust and obey, for there's no other way*
> *To be happy in Jesus, but to trust and obey.*

There is nothing like impressing Christ with our trust and obedience. Solution always comes for those who can submit their wills to the will of God. I mean those who are ready to fully obey the Lord even when it does not make any sense. Sometimes God does not make sense to your senses. Sometimes God's way of solving your problem is very ridiculous. It may look ridiculous, but it is miraculous.

Do you know what He wants you to do and are you doing what He wants you to do?

It is a pity that many people would do what men tell them to do than what God tells them. They are willing to obey men, rather than God. They are willing to follow men's methods, rather than God's methods. Who are you impressing, people, men, or Christ? Are you doing what He tells you to do or what people tell you to do?

"Do whatever he tells you" - Mary informed them that Jesus is not interested in wishing, dreaming, thinking about it, confessing, or willing, but in doing. The solution to life's problem is in doing and not in folding your arms. God is always looking for doing people and not wishing people. Unless you do it nothing will happen for you....

What must they do or what must you do? "**Whatever He tells you...**" Not whatever I tell you. Many people are doing what they are told and not what God has told them. Whatever man says to you must always be a confirmation of what God has told you. Is what you are doing what God told you or what someone told you? I have heard people saying that God has told me to do this when God did not - only their feelings told them. They mistake and equate their feelings with the voice of God. God will never tell you something that is contrary to His will... and His Word. Has He ever told you anything? Sometimes what He tells you may not make sense, *but there is always sense in God's nonsense*. Does God make sense to you?

Sometimes He does not... Why? It is because of your nonsense. Mary knew that His solution or suggestion may not be popular, may be outdated, may have become old school, may not be technological, may not be scientific, may not be psychological, may not be conservative, and may not be liberal. But, He will tell you something if you are ready and willing to do it...

Invention

"Nearby stood six stone water jars, the kind used by the Jews for ceremonial washing, each holding from twenty to thirty gallons. Jesus said to the servants, "Fill the jars with water," so they filled them to the brim. Then he told them, 'Now draw some out and take it to the master of the banquet.' They did so"... [vs. 6-8]

To invent means to do or create something new, different, and unique. Until now Jesus has not said anything to them. They have invested so much, materially and financially, into the wedding ceremony; and now is the time for spiritual invention. It is the time to try something new and different. Here is the time to take steps of faith. Here is the time to put faith into action. Unless you put your faith to work, it will never work for you. This is not the time to reason, to calculate, to argue but to put faith to work. Sometimes when you have done all that you know how to do and nothing happens, then you have to put your faith into action. You have to take some radical steps of faith.

These guys were waiting for His direction. They wanted to know what he would want them to do. May be you have been praying and wanting to know what He wants you to do that will bring a solution to that problem in your life. Don't let anybody deceive you again. The solution is right there with you.

But why the pots? The pots were what were available. There must be something that is available for you and in you. Here is the truth: *God will use what is available for you to provide what is not available for you.*

The Lord has opened our eyes to something here: God can turn ordinary things in your life into extraordinary solutions for your life. You are not far from your solution only if you can see by faith and act by faith. Here is what they had, "**Nearby stood six stone water jars, the kind used by the Jews for ceremonial washing, each holding from twenty to thirty gallons.**"

Remember this, all the six stone water pots have become empty because their water had been used by the guests at the wedding. Sometimes, God wants you to come to the point of emptiness and brokenness before He can refill you again. You must be in the state of readiness for divine manifestation. The pots were ready. The pots were ready for the potter. He told the servants to do 2 things if they expected a great manifestation to happen.

They were to *"Fill the jars with water."*

This is going to be a strenuous and tedious work. Jesus was invited to help, but it seems He was adding to the problem. Not at all. You must be ready to go through His process if you want to experience His breakthrough. Where would they get water to fill 180 gallons? They had to look for water around. They had to leave their comfort zone and fill the pots with water. Sometimes, the Lord will make you sweat before He will make things sweet for you. They were to go through the period of sowing in tears before there would be period of harvest of manifestation. The water in the jars was meant for the use of others. The servants were willing to fill the pots with water again. Even though it was very hard to do, but they were willing to try again. They were willing to do whatever Jesus told them to do that will bring joy back to the marriage ceremony.

However, they were ready to do something new…, something that was different to how things were being done before. Sometimes what you need is to be inventive and intuitive. You need to do something different if you want to experience something different. Hear the words again, *"…fill the jars with water."* This shows that, you have to fill your pots with water before your water can turn to wine. Miracles don't just happen,… you have to fill the jars… do what will bring the solution to your life. God must have something to work upon in your life and God must have something to respond to in your life. It is not praying alone, but doing as well.

Why the pots of water?

These pots of water were useful before, but they have become abandoned because they were no more useful. Their usefulness was for ceremonial washing… for the guests who came to the wedding. The pots have been used and dumped because they were not relevant in the wedding. Here is the truth: You can become irrelevant in life if you don't add relevance to your life. You can become devalued in life if you don't add value to your life.

Sometimes, your former value or relevance may become irrelevant as life progresses… Jesus decided to put and add value or relevance back to the pots. They were to fill the jars with fresh and new water. How much of fresh and new water do you put in your jars or pots? What is the condition of your spiritual pots, academic pots, vocational pots, marital pots, family pots, relationship pots, financial pots, emotional pots? Are you filling them with fresh and new waters or with - complaint, bitterness, sadness, blaming, regret, depression, discouragement, or what? Begin to invest in your life, in your present, and in your future. Don't be tired of filling your jars. In fact don't abandon your jars for another person's jars. What are you investing in your life, your present, and your future? Are you investing the right thing or the wrong thing? God will only work with what you input or put into your life. Remember this: If Jesus is what you input then solution will be your output.

They were to... *"draw some out and take it to the master of the banquet."*

They moved from doing to sharing. This is another practical step to solution. That is part of invention. They were to draw it out by faith and took it to the master of ceremony without tasting it. Sometimes, you don't need to feel it, smell it, taste it, or touch it before you will believe. There are virtues in you which must be drawn out. There are qualities in you which must be drawn out. You must be willing and ready to draw it out. Don't let your present situations kill your dreams, your passion, your purpose, your ambition, and your hope.

You must be ready to draw it out. There is a new wine in you. There is a solution in you. There is a purpose in you. There is something that is unusual in you. There is something which the world and destiny is waiting for in you. Why the master of ceremony and not the celebrants? It is for verification. It is for attestation. It is for testimony. Jesus wanted the solution to be announced by the most important person at the wedding party, the master of ceremony. The Lord gave them a **creative solution** rather than **drive through solution**. This was the first miracle of

Jesus. It was unusual. None like this has ever happened. The Lord can do such in your life. Hear what verses 9 and 10 say about the outcome of this creative solution:

> "…..and the master of the banquet tasted the water that had been turned into wine. He did not realize where it had come from, though the servants who had drawn the water knew. Then he called the bridegroom aside [10] and said, 'Everyone brings out the choice wine first and then the cheaper wine after the guests have had too much to drink, but you have saved the best till now".

It was the best wine. Let's look at the quantity of this wine mathematically:

- 6 pots of about 30 gallons each equal to 180 gallons
- 1 gallon is equal to approximate 4 liters
- 180 gallons will equal to 720 liters
- 720 liters will equal to 720,000 milliliters
- 1 bottle of wine is equal to 750 milliliters
- Therefore, 720,000 ML is equal to 960 bottles of 750 milliliters wine
- That is, 80 dozens of bottles (or 80 cartons).

But why the master of ceremony again? Hear this: the master of ceremony attested to the quality of their invention and solution. The wine must be tasted by him so that he could announce the outcome. Sometimes you need the master of ceremony in your life to announce you, to advertise you, to promote you, and to introduce you. No one would believe the servants, Mary, the hosts and even Jesus that something different has taken place. They would only believe and listen to the professional wine taster known as the master of ceremony. Who do you share your new ideas with? Do you have promoters or demoters in your life?

You will need a "master of ceremony" in your life to promote you, announce you, introduce you, and connect you. Remember that the chief butler announced the gift of Joseph to Pharaoh. Remember that John the Baptist introduced Jesus to the people. Remember that Queen Esther promoted Mordecai. You need to pray that God will link you with someone who will link you with your purpose in life. You need to also pray that God will connect you with someone or those who will promote and announce you in life.

Verse 11 of John chapter 2 says, *"This, the first of His signs (miracles, wonderworks), Jesus performed in Cana of Galilee, and manifested His glory [by it He displayed His greatness and His power openly], and His disciples believed in Him [adhered to, trusted in, and relied on Him]."* [Amplfied]

Yours may not be a physical wedding ceremony. It may be a particular thing in your life that is suffering defeat and setback. May be your wine has gone. Your peace has gone. Your happiness has gone. Your testimony has gone. The Lord can still bring back and bring out the best out of your worst. He can manifest His glory in your story. He can turn your story to glory. He is the Lord of solution. What you need to do is to Invite Him, Inform Him, Involve Him, Impress Him, and Invest Him.

CHAPTER SIX

You Have to Go Through Stages of Divine Making

"If God does not begin it, He cannot maintain it. If God does not maintain it, He cannot complete it. If God does not make you, You cannot make it."

This topic is based on the instruction given by God to Prophet Jeremiah. Here God likens His working in our lives to how a potter works on the clay. The potter's working place is always full of horrible and unexpected things. There is a chisel, knives, hammers, water, coloring, apron, table, and so on. At times it looks meaningless and disappointing, but something is going to come out of it.

This is how divine making looks like. This is how it looks like when God is making you. You cannot be a finished product if you do not go through making. That is to say, if your life will become something it must go through something.

It is sad to note that many people are not products of God's making; they are products of man's making. They are what people have made them to be. They are what situations have made them to become. They are what friends or peer pressures have made them to be. Some are what their spouses have made them to be. Many people are what the society has made them to be. Some are what the church has made them to be. But what has God made you to be? Has God made you or you are the one making yourself? It is when God makes you that you can make it. Here are the facts:

- Unless God makes your job or career you cannot make it.
- Unless God makes your marriage you cannot make it.
- Unless God makes your spouse you cannot make it.
- Unless God makes your life you cannot make it.
- Unless God makes your children you cannot make them.
- Unless God makes it happen in your life you cannot make it.

This is the truth of Jeremiah 18:1-6. You can only return it back to Apple for the repair or replacement of your IPad only if it was made by Apple. This is where many people miss it. They want God to maintain, sustain, and fix what He did not begin and make. What a waste of time. Even though God made all things, but He did not make everything. Therefore, from the passage of Jeremiah 18:1-6 we shall examine the stages of divine making.

Processing

"So I went down to the potter's house, and I
saw him working at the wheel."[v.3]

The word processing here has the idea of continuity. The phrase, *"I saw him working at the wheel,"* shows that God has not stopped working at the wheel. The wheel is an unstable, shaking, disturbing, and chaotic movement. The wheel is always rolling and spinning. The wheel is not balanced. The wheel looks out of control. The wheel looks ugly. When the wheel looks this way, it shows that the potter is at work at the wheel. The potter is making something.

The Lord is the potter and we are the clay that God is working on at the wheel. God is always working 24/7 on the wheel. He is always working 24/7 on our lives. He is always fixing something. And whenever God is working something out in our lives, sometimes it will look as if nothing is working out in our lives.

Sometimes, when your life is out of control is when God is in the control. The process of making will require wheeling, spinning, and rolling. You will be dislocated, disappointed, and even defeated. Sometimes, a period of peace and tranquility will come when you will begin to give testimonies and laugh; then comes another spinning and processing for another level.

The spinning and processing time is not a good time. Sometimes it is long, and sometimes it is short. It is a period of crying, weeping, defeating, hopelessness, and uncertainty. You will feel as if God has abandoned you or closed the heavens on you. You will feel as if your prayers are not answered by God again. You will only tolerate God by faith. Your faith will become shaken and unstable. You are going through a process on the wheel.

Have you even been to the place where things are being made or repaired? It takes more patience and waiting to make or repair. It requires a slow process. You can never be a unique product or result in life unless you go through a process. Ask Abraham; ask Noah; ask Joseph; ask Daniel; and ask Jesus Christ. They all went through wheel of process.

Every finished product must go through process. Every meaningful and useful thing in life must go through process. The processing period is the time when things are shapeless, purposeless, and even meaningless. It is the beginning stage. This is the **preparation stage.**

If the Lord is going to make you to make it in life, you will have to go through the period of processing. This is the preparation stage. The stage when you will be nobody. The stage when you will be nothing. The stage when you will be broken and pruned by the Lord. This is the period when you will be placed on the wheel of His will. It is a time where His will is replaced with your will on the wheel. It is on the wheel that His purpose takes over your purpose, and His plans take over your plan.

It is the time of processing that the Lord makes known His purpose in your life. This is the time when you will know what you are meant to be. It is the time when God makes all thing to work together for good according to His purpose for your life. This is when you will know who you are and what you are destined to be. The wheel is the wheel of preparation and identity.

Whenever you are going through processing you will know. Don't try to dodge processing. Your processing time may be your education, your waiting on God for a job, your waiting on God for a relationship, your waiting on God for something. This is the time that God must work on you before things would work for you. You must be ready to go through the processing time if you want to make it in life. Don't rush to appear in life. If you appear too soon you will disappear too soon. You need processing.

Shaping

"But the pot he was shaping from the clay
was marred in his hands..." [v.4a]

The word "shaping" has the idea of configuring or structuring something to meet a specific design or model. The material that is being used by the potter is clay; the product to be made by the potter is a pot or vessel; the method to be used by the potter is shaping. The potter has in mind the type or prototype of vessel or pot that he wanted to shape or mold the clay into. Only the potter knows. He has the original sketch and design with him. **The potter works by design and not by default**.

However, our text says that the vessel or pot which the potter was shaping or making was spoiled, defective, and messy in his hand. I mean, in the hands of the potter. This would make people think that the potter is ineffective or inefficient. Sometimes, that is how we feel about God, as ineffective and inefficient. We ask, if God is all-powerful and caring, why did He allow things to go wrong in my life? But let us look at this verse or phrase closely to see who is with fault, whether the potter or the clay. The Amplified Bible says, *"And the vessel that he was making from clay was spoiled in the hand of the potter."* It was the vessel that the potter was making that was spoiled and not the potter. This shows that because the Lord is good and powerful does not mean that things cannot go wrong in your life even while you are still in His hands. Always remember this: *something can go wrong in your life, but God cannot go wrong.*

In my thirty years in pastoral ministry, I have seen people blaming God when things go wrong in their lives. I have seen people abandoning God and accusing Him of negligence and being ineffective. I have seen men and women backsliding because they felt God had failed them. They thought that God was careless by letting things go wrong with them. I wish only that they would find out and know that God is always at the wheel 24/7 to fix all the messes which we have caused to ourselves.

Sometimes people project their anger on God. They always make Him the scapegoat of all their predicaments. God is never the problem; the problem is the problem. The situations of life are what always cause situations that we are going through. We have to know that God is never the problem. You cannot blame Henry Ford for all the accidents of all the brands or models of General Motors. You cannot blame Bill Gates for all the viruses being experienced by Microsoft users.

But here is another truth: The fact that something goes wrong in your life is an indication that you are qualified for shaping toward divine making. He has to shape you so that you can fit the purpose for which He has created you. For God to shape you, He must trim down and cut down and remove some things from you. He must remove some stones, broken glasses, nails, and particles that have corroded your life. Shaping time is the time of trimming and fine-tuning. Many people are going through their shaping. This is the **construction stage**.

The shaping stage is when God makes you fit into His purpose and plan. Things may go wrong at this time, but God uses them to shape you. This is the time that God tests you and allows you to go through difficulties and hard times. This is the time that God wants you to be in shape for His purpose for your life. It is a tough time. It is the time when the devil would make you think that God is not good; God is evil; God is powerless; and God is ineffective. But I want you to know that God is good; He is just shaping you.

Forming

"... so the potter formed it into another pot." [v. 4b]

The Amplified Bible says, *"... so he made it over."*

There is no perfect and wonderful product that will not become defective. It is the law of production. It is the law of diminishing return. Even the best of the best will become depreciated and defective. Sometimes the best job, church, marriage, education, career, relationship and even life tends to become deformed, defective, damaged, and messed up. This is when the potter comes in, to form it into another vessel.

Did you get the revelation? The potter will redo, rework, reshape, readjust, rearrange, and restructure the pot or vessel into another type. Even if the original type or pattern has been destroyed and defective, God can form it into another vessel. Not that God cannot repair or replace, but sometimes He prefers to make another. In other words, God can make another thing for you if the former one has become destroyed and defective. Listen to what He said in Isaiah 43:18-19, *"Forget the former things; do not dwell on the past. See, I am doing a new thing! Now it springs up; do you not perceive it? I am making a way in the wilderness and streams in the wasteland."*

The potter begins all over. The potter does not give up. The potter goes back to work. The potters makes another thing out of the defective pot. This tells us that God begins all over with you and helps you to begin all over when you think that all is over,... is not over. If God says it is not over... then it is not over. Your mind may tell you that it is over. Your boss may tell you that it is over. Your physician may tell you that it is over. Your case worker may tell you that it over. Your supervisor may tell you that it is over. Your bank may tell you that is over. But remember this: they are not your Maker. It is only your Maker, the Potter, who knows your beginning and your end. It is He who can determine when it is over with you. Since He has not and since He is always at the wheel 24/7 - then it is not over for you.

God can go back to work because of you. You are the clay in His hands. He is the Potter that is working on you. He does not and will not give up on you even if everyone has given up on you. That is why you should not give up on yourself. You have a Potter who works on the wheel 24/7 and who is working on your life.

You may look defective, deformed, dejected, disappointed, disoriented, and discouraged. But He can make you all over again. He can give you a new beginning, a new hope, a new purpose, a new meaning, a new focus, a new job, a new marriage, a new relationship, a new business, a new career, a new house, and so on...

- God can bring the best out of your worst.
- God can bring a message out of your mess

- God can bring a glory out of your story
- God can bring a testimony out of your test
- God can bring a crown out of your cross
- God can bring a fame out of your shame
- God can bring a miracle out of your ridicule
- God can bring treasure out of your trash
- God can bring grace out of your disgrace

He is forming something. He is making something. Sometimes you don't feel it, you don't know it, but He is forming something. Maybe you are about to give up, to lose hope, and to lose faith. I want to assure that He is forming something.

The forming stage is the period when God is making something out of your life. It is the time when God is turning your situation around. Hear how Isaiah describes this stage in 29:16, *"You turn things upside down, as if the potter were thought to be like the clay! Shall what is formed say to the one who formed it, 'You did not make me?' Can the pot say to the potter, 'You know nothing?' "*

The New King James Version says, *"Surely you have things turned around! Shall the potter be esteemed as the clay; For shall the thing made say of him who made it, 'He did not make me?' Or shall the thing formed say of him who formed it, 'He has no understanding?'*

This is the time when God is working something in your life. This is the time that God is developing and maturing you for His making. This is the development stage. This is the **deconstruction stage**.

Redesigning

"....shaping it as seemed best to him." [v. 4c]

The Amplified Bible says, *"...reworking it into another vessel as it seemed good to the potter to make it."* The NET Bible says, *"So he would rework the clay into another kind of pot as he saw fit."*

Hear this, the Potter did not throw the clay and the pot away, but He redesigned it into another pot. God can go back to work because of you to correct what has become wrong in your life. He can redesign your life. He can redirect you. He can take you through another door if a door has been closed.

The word "redesign" means to revise in appearance, function, or content. It has to do with changing the form of something into something better. This is what God does. God can redesign your tragedy to become the strategy for your making. He can redesign your dreams, your future, your aspirations, and even the plans of your life. He redesigns your life so that it can become what is best to Him and not what is best to you. Hear what the text says, "... *shaping it as seemed best to him.*"

Best to who? It is what is best to the Potter. It is not as what or how the clay wants, but as what is the best to the Potter. Hear this: *What you think is the best to you may be the worst to God and what you think is the worst to you may be the best to God.* Sometimes we think that we know what is best for us. Not at all. Only God knows what is best for us. But we must allow Him to do the making.

This is the stage when God remodels you for His glory, showcase and manifestation. This is the stage of His final touch. This is the stage of decoration. This is stage of putting the icing on the cake. This is the period when God brings back His original glory into your life. This is the **manifestation stage.**

These four stages are the circles which God uses to recycle us for His glory. He always puts us through these four stages of making. The stages are never ending. They continue until we die. God does not stop working on you. He is always at the wheel, processing, shaping, forming, and redesigning.

CHAPTER SEVEN

Have the Working Net for Divine Networking

> *"The Lord must take you deeper before He will take you higher."*
> *"The deeper your revelation the higher your manifestation."*

Only Luke has the record of this story. It is a story that is very unique, touchy, spiritual, inspirational, and motivational. This is a story of hopelessness, helplessness, emptiness, and faithlessness. The passage records in verse 1 that after a large number of people came to Jesus, He decided to use the open space of the Sea of Galilee to teach them. At least, He did not need to pay for any dome or theater to host His free public seminar. He decided to use the open space of the Sea of Galilee.

Not that alone, He needed a boat, not a seat or pulpit, to sit and from where He would teach them. Remember this, there was no public address system; therefore, He had to find a natural means to create one. The best one He would use, which He did not have to pay for, was the sea wave. And He must sit or stand on the sea so that the sea wave can transmit or echo His voice to the hearers.

But when He got to this place, He found out that two boats were available for Him to use. But why were they available? Because the owners who were fishermen have not caught any fish and have even given up catching any. One of the boats belonged to Simon Peter and Andrew while the second to James and John, the sons of Zebedee. Jesus made use of Peter's boat for His teaching and in turn, He turned his working net to divine network. Hence, the focus of this message is Peter's working net.

Peter's working net was his fishing net. The major tool for his business. The net was his career, vocation, skill, expertise, and professionalism. Peter can never operate without this net. He was used to this net. What is your own working net? Your net may be your skill, career, certificate, license, practice, expertise, professionalism, and what you are good at. Sometimes, success is not about what you are good at or how many connections you have. It is about God or divine network or connection. In other words, success in life is about what God makes out of your skill, ability, education, certificate, license, and so on.

Then what are the characteristics of a net or working net that will be turned to divine network? Or how can God turn your working net (your job, skill, ability, business etc.) into His network for more results? For this to happen, the following must characterize your net as based on Luke 5:1-11.

Renewed Net

"He saw at the water's edge two boats, left there by the fishermen, who were <u>washing their nets</u>" [v. 2]

Why were they washing the nets? It was because they had worked all night continuously and did not catch any fish except a great deal of soils, stones, debris, and filthiness. Therefore, they were cleaning their nets, in order to lay them up and did not want to make any further attempts lest they experience the same result. They were disappointed, discouraged, distressed, and disturbed. We don't know how long they have been using this net, may be very long. This net was their major tool for catching fish. This net was their secret. This net had delivered fish in the past. But this net had failed to deliver fish again. Then what is happening to this net? Why has this net disappointed them today? They have the skills to catch fish, but the net was not cooperating. What happens when your skills do not match up with your results? That is to say, what happens when your opportunity cannot measure up with your ability? Or what happens when what has been bringing you more success in life is no more bringing any success, but failure?

Sometimes this is what happens to investors, businessmen and women, students, civil servants, employers, and so on. We are always used to using to the same net with the same result; the same method with the same result; the same program with the same result; and the same approach with the same result; and the same people with the same result.

In economics, there is what we call "the laws of diminishing returns." The laws of diminishing returns state that after a certain point (called the point of diminishing returns), additional input to a system of production will produce less and less output. This is what happened here, and it can happen to anybody and to us in this life. Peter and his friends' nets were experiencing the law of diminishing returns. Sometimes, ministers, leaders, pastors, and workers, businessmen and women, students, professionals, employees, and do on can reach the point of diminishing returns when the end does not justify the means or when there is a setback in result or output.

But what did they do to those nets? The Bible says that they were *"washing their nets."* Wow!

- They did not discard or throw away the nets.
- They did not trade the nets.

- They did not junk the nets.
- They did not trash the nets.
- They did not abandon the nets.
- They did not pawn the nets.
- They did not destroy the nets.

...as many people would have done.

Instead, they still believed that they could still add value to these nets. That is to say that, even though the nets have become devalued, they knew that were still valuable. That was why they were "**washing the nets.**" They were washing the nets for another use. They knew that the nets could still become relevant, but must be washed. The nets must be renewed. The nets must be cleansed. The nets must be cleaned. The nets had contained and gathered stones, debris, woods, broken glasses, and all sorts of ugly objects. They must be removed. The nets must be renewed.

Spiritual renewal is necessary for everyone who expects his/her vocational, social, spiritual, biological, marital, and financial net to be linked with a God-divine network. Sometimes we will become dried, depleted, and burnt-out spiritually, emotionally, physically, psychologically, and even financially. This happens as a result of many things in our lives. It always affects our productivity and result. It is dangerous to continue the work when you are no more productive. What do we need? We need spiritual renewal and we need to remove some things out of our systems. We need to check and remove whatever that is clogging our operational wheels as well as results.

The Message Bible says that they *"were out scrubbing their nets."* We need spiritual scrubbing before we can function more effectively for the Lord. Many have become corroded, eroded, and polluted in their minds. No wonder their nets do not catch any fish again. Brethren, we need spiritual scrubbing. Let us read:

Hebrew 10:22:

"Let us draw near to God with a sincere heart and with the full assurance that faith brings, having our hearts sprinkled to cleanse us from a guilty conscience and having our bodies washed with pure water."

John 15: 2

"Any branch in Me that does not bear fruit [that stops bearing] He cuts away (trims off, takes away); and He cleanses and repeatedly prunes every branch that continues to bear fruit, to make it bear more and richer and more excellent fruit." [Amplified]

Remember that:

➤ Ruth washed and cleansed herself before she went to Boaz.
➤ Esther also washed and perfumed herself before she appeared before the King.
➤ The Old Testament priests washed themselves and their garments before ministering to the Lord.
➤ Isaiah was purified before he was commissioned for the work of God.

Therefore, the Lord also expects us to be a renewed net or vessel every day and every time if we are going to function for His glory. No wonder, the apostle appeals in Romans 12:1-2: *"I beseech you therefore, brethren, by the mercies of God, that you present your bodies a living sacrifice, holy, acceptable to God, which is your reasonable service. ²And do not be conformed to this world, but be transformed by the renewing of your mind, that you may prove what is that good and acceptable and perfect will of God."* This washing or renewing must be everyday... Your net must be a renewed net to qualify it for divine network.

If God is to connect you with a greater opportunity, blessing, job, and relationship, you must be a renewed, dedicated, uncompromised, unpolluted net or vessel in His hand.

Revealed Net

"When he had finished speaking, he said to Simon, 'Put out into deep water, and let down the nets for a catch.' " [v. 4, NIV]

"When He had stopped speaking, He said to Simon (Peter), 'Put out into the deep [water], and lower your nets for a haul.' " [Amplified]

"When he had finished speaking, he said to Simon, 'Now go out where it is deeper, and let down your nets to catch some fish.' " [New Living Translation]

Let us pause for a while. Before this time in verse 3, the Bible says, *"He got into one of the boats, the one belonging to Simon, and asked him to put out a little from shore. Then he sat down and taught the people from the boat."* [NIV] The Message Bible says, *"He climbed into the boat that was Simon's and asked him to put out a little from the shore. Sitting there, using the boat for a pulpit, he taught the crowd."*

He did not even ask Peter why he was washing his net, nor showed any concern about his frustration for not catching any fish. He only got to the boat of Peter without asking for his permission, but asked him to push it to the middle of the water. Some versions of the Bible say that He commanded Peter, saying, *"Carry ye the ship from dry land a little into the sea."* How would you feel if you were Peter? How would you answer Jesus or what would have been your reaction? To bring it home, what do you do with God when you are frustrated? What do you do with God when you are disappointed? It was after Peter met His need that

He decided to meet his need also. Unless you meet His need, He cannot meet your need.

Not that the Lord Jesus did not have concern for Peter; He wanted to test his obedience before He would network with him. There must be something for the Lord to respond to in your life. His intervention is always based on your investment of faith. In verse 4, the Lord gave him a revelation that would solve his frustration. Hear the revelation:

> *"Put out into deep water, and let down the nets for a catch."* [NIV]

> *"Now go out where it is deeper, and let down your nets to catch some fish."* [The Message Bible]

Here the Lord told Peter to change his strategy and method of fishing. He was to go out to where it is deeper. Peter must take a risk before something will happen. Peter must take a step ahead of others before he can be ahead of others. He must go deeper and not on the surface. The surface is the level of sight, but the deeper is the level of revelation. It is on the level that you operate in life that will determine your result, output, and effectiveness. If you operate on the surface, you will not catch more. Or you may only catch what is on the surface. However, if you operate in the level of revelation, the deeper level, you will catch more... How deep are you with God? Hear what the Psalmist says in Psalms 42:1: *"As the deer pants for streams of water, so my soul pants for you, my God."* Hear this: *the deeper your revelation, the higher your manifestation.*

Peter was to act on revelation and not on information. All this while, Peter has been acting and working on information. His methods and tactics had been based on the latest information about the Sea of Galilee logistics in regards to fishing. But the Lord told him to change his method by giving him revelation. Information will only give an idea on how to run it, but revelation will give a solution. Revelation is deeper insight into what you are doing.

Peter was told to move from the natural realm to the supernatural realm. The deeper level is the secret place of the Most High. It is the level of what eyes have not seen and ears have not heard. It is the level of faith. Hebrews 11:1: "Faith is the confidence that what we hope for will actually happen; it gives us assurance about things we cannot see." [The New Living Translation] Hebrews 11:3: "By faith we understand that the entire universe was formed at God's command, that what we now see did not come from anything that can be seen." [NLT]

Peter was to move away from the ordinary to the extraordinary. Sometimes, you need to move away from them at the surface, so that you can connect or enter into divine network. **The Lord must take you deeper before He will take you higher**.

This is where we are going. The real revelation is this statement, *"and let down the nets for a catch."* What nets? You mean the same nets or new nets? The Lord was very direct and particular. The same nets. These were the ordinary nets that have failed to catch anything before, but have become extraordinary nets. The nets have now become revelation nets. They were the revealed nets. The nets that have been renewed have now become the nets that have been revealed as the chosen nets. Oh I wish and pray that God will reveal to you the power that is in your net. Jesus saw what Peter did not see in the nets.

- Jesus saw potentials
- Jesus saw abilities
- Jesus saw effectiveness
- Jesus saw efficiency
- Jesus saw usefulness
- Jesus saw magnetic power
- Jesus saw many fishes

What did you see in your net? What are you seeing in your net? What have you seen in your net?

This is beyond reasoning. This is revelation. That the stone which the builder once rejected will become the head of the corner? You may feel or think that you are dirty, dejected, irrelevant, messy, messed up, unqualified, disqualified, and useless. But you are not if you can align your life and surrender your life to Jesus. Maybe you have given up on your net thinking that nothing can happen again. The Lord is saying to you again: let down the nets for a catch. It is no more an ordinary net, but a revelation and extraordinary net. The word of the Lord has entered into the nets and they have become revelation nets. They are no more dried nets. They are no more dried bones nets. Today, I want you to speak and command your nets to hear the Word of God and come to life. Speak the Word of God into your life. I prophesy life into your net. I prophesy hope into your net. I prophesy effectiveness and great result into your net. I pray that the Lord will give you revelation and open your eyes to know or see where you will launch your net to for a catch. Amen...

Released Net

"Simon answered, 'Master, we've worked hard all night and haven't caught anything. But because you say so, I will let down the nets.' " [v. 5, NIV]

"And Simon (Peter) answered, 'Master, we toiled all night [[a] exhaustingly] and caught nothing [in our nets]. But on the ground of Your word, I will lower the nets [again].' " [Amplified]

The working net for divine network must be a released net. Peter gave excuses why he thought it was useless to make use of his nets at this time. Firstly, they have used the nets a lot... "We've worked hard." That is, I am tired of trying. I am tired of using the nets again. We have put all our efforts and energies into the use of the nets. It is better to keep the nets somewhere. Sometimes you feel that you don't want to do anything again mostly after you have tried hard and nothing has happened. This is when many people want to fold or pack their nets... They don't want to try again. Like Peter, they are tired emotionally, psychologically, physically, and spiritually. They have become exhausted... Have you?

Secondly, they have used the nets at the right and appropriate time *"all night"* and cannot be used in the afternoon. The best time to fish is in the evening and not in the afternoon. We have used all our professional strategies and resources and cannot catch anything. Many people have done everything and yet, no or little results. They have done all that they know how to do at the time which they think is the right time. They now feel that time is no more on their side... Have you?

Thirdly, the nets have not produced anything *"caught nothing."* What Peter is saying here is that we have done all that we are gifted and skillful at doing and yet there is no result. Maybe you are also saying that I have done all that I know how to do, all that I have been trained, educated, or licensed to do, and all that I am best at doing, but there has not been any result in my life. Hear this, the nets have not produced anything in their hands because the nets have not been connected with divine network. The same principle is applicable to you and to your net. Unless your net is connected with divine authorization and revelation, it cannot produce anything. Let us listen to Peter as he connected his nets to divine network:

"But because you say so, I will let down the nets." [NIV]

"But on the ground of Your word, I will lower the nets [again]." [Amplified]

Peter decided to release the nets to the revelation of the word of the Lord. Before he has been "casting" the nets, but now, he was ready to "lower or let down the nets." That is, he was ready to release his nets, that is, his systems, strategies, resources, tactics, methods, approaches, skills, potentials, and expertise to the word of God. Peter is saying, what use are they to us if we don't release them to your word.

Brothers and sisters, you need to release yourself, your passion, your frustration, your skills, your abilities, your gifts, and everything to the Lord so that He can maximize you. Stop arguing with God. Stop showing that you know it all. Stop focusing on how best you are. Stop complaining about what you are unable to do. Stop complaining...

- Abraham had to release his Isaac for greater blessing.
- Moses had to release his staff and status to God for greater use by God.
- Joseph had to release his robe to temptation to achieve his greatness.
- Hannah had to release Samuel to the Lord to be mothers of other children.
- The 12 disciples had to release all for the sake of following Christ.
- The widow had to release all her mites before she could be recognized by Jesus.
- The widow of Zarephat had to release her last meal to Elijah to get blessed.
- The Shunemite woman had to release her house to Elisha to be blessed with a child.
- The small boy had to release his bread and fish to feed more than 5000 people.

Brothers and sister, *if you don't release it you cannot receive it.*

Rewarded Net

"When they had done so, they caught such a large number
of fish that their nets began to break." [v. 6, NIV]

This is the outcome of divine networking: great reward. Divine networking always brings rewards. Two rewards are mentioned in this verse.

The first is: *"They caught such a large number of fish."* This must be the first time they would catch such a great amount of fish. How many? The Bible says, a large number. Divine network is not only demanding, as seen in steps 1 to 3, it is also rewarding. When you connect your nets with the Lord, He will give you large numbers of fish.

This is the level or realm when there is no more effort, labor, and struggle. It is just divine connection or network. When you are connected with God, He will connect you with results... God's connection is the key to your promotion, distinction, and manifestation.

This is what the Lord said to Zerubbabel: *"Then he said to me, 'This is what the Lord says to Zerubbabel: It is not by force nor by strength, but by my Spirit, says the Lord of Heaven's Armies.' "* [Zech. 4:6, NLT]. The Lord further said in Psalms 127:1: *"Unless the Lord builds the house, the builders labor in vain."*

The only person who can bring unexpected, unprecedented, and exponential result into your life is God Himself. Paul said in 1 Corinthians 3:6-7: *"I planted the seed, Apollos watered it, but God has been making it grow. So neither the one who plants nor the one who waters is anything, but only God, who makes things grow."* If you are a minister or pastor, it is only God who can grow your church. If you are a businessman or woman, it is only God who can grow your business. If you are a student, it is only God who can bring the best result. If you are a career/professional man or woman, it is only God who can reward you. Hebrews 11:6 calls God the "Rewarder" of those who diligently seek Him.

Brothers and sister, you can only try, only God can bring result. It is not what you do or what you know or what you know how to do, it is what the Lord can do or will do. Hear this: *God can do in a day what you cannot do in many years.* What you need to do is to allow Him to do it. Don't struggle to use our nets. Don't struggle to catch the fish. Let God...

The second thing is this, "*... their nets began to break.*" Wow! This is incredible. In a day, in a moment, in a second, in a minute, and in a period, they went from emptiness to fullness, failure to success, and nothing to something. Their working nets could not contain the result which divine networking has brought to them. I pray that the Lord will answer your prayers more than your expectations... I also pray that He will open the windows of heaven and pour His blessings upon your life that your containers will not be able to contain them. Amen.

However, hear this, don't let your achievement and status get into your head, rather let it break you. The verse says, "*... their nets began to break.*" Spiritually, this means brokenness. You have to be broken for God so that He can fill you more. Hear what verse 7 says, I love it, "*They signaled to their partners in the other boat to come and take hold with them. And they came and filled both the boats, so that they began to sink.*" [Amplified]. They knew that even though their nets were full, they still needed the help of others. Only a broken person would see himself or herself as not having it all. Don't be too full of yourself that you think that you don't need others. You need good people in your life and around you if you want to excel in life. You need partners who will help you become owners... Right partnership is the gateway to right ownership.

Always remember that nobody can do the work of God alone. Nobody can succeed in the work of God alone. Nobody can get to the top alone. Nobody can succeed in business alone. Nobody can make it in academics alone. Nobody can get there alone...

There must be collaboration and completion, but not competition. That your net catches the fish does not mean that you don't need others. Sometimes, though the farmer plants alone and the sower sows alone, but he will need more workers or laborers to harvest the field. What happens when your season of harvest comes? Do you have the right people around to help you with your harvest? Do you have the right and necessary networking to network your harvest? Are you ready for the great result that is coming your way?

There is nothing that can be compared with divine networking. But always remember that it is always and only available for you when you have a working net. What is your working net?

CHAPTER EIGHT

Avoid Things That Hinder Completion

> *"It is YOU who can hinder YOU."*

Why do people fail to complete what they began? Why am I finding it difficult to complete or succeed at something or anything? Is it the devil? The answer is no. Is it witches and witchcrafts? The answer is no. Is it my enemies? The answer is no. Then what is it? **IT IS YOU**.

The power to succeed and complete whatever we began in life resides in us. God did not create us incompletely. He has designed us completely and successfully. That is why He has put the power to complete whatever we began in us. That is why nobody can stop you in life unless you stop yourself. You are your worst enemy. You are your best enemy. Your life is like a car. The car will only move when you press the gas. The car will only stop when you press the break. Therefore, you have the power to move and to stop your life. In fact, you will determine the speed of your life.

Sometimes we blame people and society for our inability to complete what we began in life. Often times we blame God, our parents, our spouses, and our makeups. We blame our color, our accents, our background, our status, our culture, our systems, and our (you fill in the blank) for why we are unable to complete successfully what we began in life. Many have dropped out of school because of what and how they feel about themselves.

Sometimes, people focus on the wrong sides and wrong reasons on why they are unable to complete something in life. From the story we read in Luke 9:57-62, Jesus shows us that failure to complete in life is not the reason which many consider as the reason. Jesus' thesis from this story is this: *It is you who can hinder you.* Therefore, from Luke 9:57-62, let us examine from this passage things that hinder people from completing what they began in life. They are three things, all beginning from the letter **C.**

Convenience

"As they were walking along the road, a man said to him, 'I will follow you wherever you go.' Jesus replied, 'Foxes have dens and birds have nests, but the Son of Man has no place to lay his head.' "[vs. 57-58]

The first excuse of this man is this: **Will it be convenient for me?**

Success or excellent in life always begins with decision. You have to decide before you begin. This is what we see in the life of this man. He decided to follow Jesus always, until the end. That is what so many people have done; they have made a decision to serve and follow Jesus. This is the same about major things in our lives. They all begin with decision. That is, a decision has to be made. You have to decide to do whatever you want to do in life. It is one thing to pray, it is another thing to decide. God will never decide for you. God will guide you, but He will not decide for you.

- You have to decide to marry that person.
- You have to decide to take up that job.
- You have to decide to go into that business.
- You have to decide to go into the college.
- You have to decide to pursue that degree program.
- You have to decide to go into that relationship.

Life is about decisions. If you fail to decide in life you will be put aside in life. However, decision does not guarantee completion. Many people have decided and have even begun, but are unable to complete. They wonder why they are unable to complete what they began despite their resolute decisions. The sad thing is that some people are yet to decide about what they want to complete and accomplish in their lives. The first major hindrance and reason for inability to decide as well as to complete what we have decided is CONVENIENCE. So many people have not decided or have given up because they think it is not convenient. Convenience has been defined as a quality or situation that makes something easy or useful for someone by reducing the amount of work or time required to do something. Or, something that makes you more comfortable or allows you to do things more easily.

The man in our text wanted or decided to follow Jesus until the end, but he was concerned about his comfort and convenience. But Jesus told him that convenience will keep him away from following Him until end. Convenience is:

- Expecting the gain without preparing for the pain
- Expecting the crown without preparing for the cross
- Expecting to be star without preparing for the scars
- Expecting the sweetness without preparing for the sweating
- Expecting the betterment without preparing for the bitterness

The problem is that many people have abandoned or given up on their decisions, focuses, visions, and ambitions in life just because of the present comfort or enjoyment. They have stopped dreaming, focusing, pressing on, trying, and aiming in life because they are not ready to inconvenience themselves. They want to begin it or complete it, but only when it is convenient for them. Many have stopped trying because it is not convenient for them. Dear readers...

- Don't let the present income you are making stop you from completing.
- Don't let the little help you are receiving from the government stop you from completing.
- Don't let the little job you are doing stop you from completing.
- Don't let your marriage stop you from completing.
- Don't let your childbearing stop you from completing.
- Don't let your status stop you from completing.
- Don't be too comfortable to complete what you began.

There is no convenient and comfortable time to begin or complete something. This is what Jesus told this man. The man was willing to follow Jesus. But Jesus knew what was in his heart, that he could not handle inconvenience. To this, Jesus said, *"Jesus replied, 'Foxes have dens and birds have nests, but the Son of Man has no place to lay his head.'"* [NIV] Hear how the message Bible puts it, *"Are you ready to rough it? We're not staying in the best inns, you know."* You must be ready to go through before you enjoy breakthrough. So many people want to excel or successful in life, but they are not willing to pay the price. They don't want to go through, but they want to enjoy breakthrough. They are not willing to rough it.

Sometimes in life, you have to be ready to suspend present enjoyment to endure present pain, so that you can fully enjoy the future enjoyment. That is why you don't allow the present enjoyment to jeopardize your future enjoyment. You have to practice what is called "delayed gratification." This is suspending the gratification of present desires, so that you can achieve your future desire. You must be ready to inconvenience yourself. Great men and women who are successful and excellent in life inconvenienced themselves at one point of their life. The following was said about Moses in Hebrews 11:24-27:

> [24] *"By faith Moses, when he had grown up, refused to be known as the son of Pharaoh's daughter.* [25] *He chose to be mistreated along with the people of God rather than to enjoy the fleeting pleasures of sin.* [26] *He regarded disgrace for the sake of Christ as of greater value than the treasures of Egypt, because he was looking ahead to his reward.* [27] *By faith he left Egypt, not fearing the king's anger; he persevered because he saw him who is invisible."* (NIV)

Therefore, don't wait until things are alright for you before you will begin what you need to begin in life. There is no convenient time. There is no convenient place either. Hear what Solomon said in Ecclesiastes 11:4: *"Whoever watches the wind will not plant; whoever looks at the clouds will not reap."* Don't wait until it is convenient for you, start now.

Concern

> *"He said to another man, 'Follow me.' But he replied,*
> *'Lord, first let me go and bury my father.' Jesus said*
> *to him, 'Let the dead bury their own dead, but you go*
> *and proclaim the kingdom of God.' "[vs. 59-60]*

The second excuse of this man: **Who will take care of what I have been taken care of?**

Did you hear that? Unlike the first man who decided to follow Jesus, our Lord Jesus Christ Himself invited this man to follow Him. But this man was full of worries and anxieties. Listen to what the man said, *"Lord, first let me go and bury my father."* His concern was seen in something else and not in giving his totality (all) to Jesus. Whatever you are concerned about will be your worries in life, and whatever you worry about will become your focus in life. Worry or concern will hinder you from either beginning or completing in life.

This man was so concerned about being the messiah of his family that he missed the most important thing for his life. His father was still living; his father was old. He wanted to delay his call and invitation to follow Jesus until his father's burial and the will and inheritance was taken care of before coming to follow Jesus. He was focusing on the NOW and forgot the THEN. He was concerned about what he could see now and forgot what he could not see in the future.

Excuse me, there is nothing wrong in taking care of others that are around you and in your life. But remember this, *"It is when you are better that you will help others better."* If you don't better yourself, others around you cannot be better. I have discovered that many people have developed a messiah complex that they see themselves as the care providers to all their relatives and friends and thereby forget to take care of themselves. Or, they have abandoned their pursuit in life to take care of others around them. They believe and assume that if they do not do it, no one can do it… messiah complex!

Many teenagers or young adults who should still be under the care of their parents are going through what is known as "parentification" and "sandwich generation" because they are the ones taking care of their parents and other siblings. Many have abandoned their dreams, visions, and plans for their future all in the name of helping others. Many cannot go to college or a university because they have to take care of their parents and siblings. Some have dropped out of school, work, business, and lucrative professions because they have to take care of their aging parents and younger siblings. This is very common in the African community and mostly in Nigeria.

The majority of immigrant Africans who are living in United States of America and other Western countries are toiling, laboring, struggling, and working hard 24/7 in order to take care of parents and sibling whom they left at home. As a result, many of them cannot realize and maximize their potentials because they have to do whatever it takes to care of their folks at home. They are worried, anxious, troubled, and overwhelmed and have abandoned all what they have begun to better their future because they have to deal with the present pressures from home. No wonder many are ending up in life like their parents! They are dysfunctional; they are unfulfilled; they are entangled in drugs; they are confused and they are fraudulent. They want to meet the demands and pressures from home.

Unless you are an emigrant or immigrant from Africa, you may not understand what I am saying. Every member of your family (nucleus and extended) looks on you as the savior and messiah of the family. They will expect you to do everything for them. You will be expected to pay your siblings' school fees, build a house for your parents, and provide for all your uncles, nieces, nephews, and aunties. They will call you even if you don't call them. You will be known at MoneyGram or Western Union centers. What can you do, avoid them? This is a great concern to many of us who are from Africa.

Here is one thing about concern or worry, it usually leads to anxiety and anxiety will lead to fear. You must also remember that you cannot solve all problems. Before you can solve the problems of others you have to solve yours first, which is, complacency and inability to begin and complete what you began. Before you can help others, you have to help yourself first. I know that this is very difficult for many of my colleagues who are from Africa. I have seen many of my church members dropping out of school or unable to go back to school here in the USA because of their concern for their families in Africa. Here is what I use to tell them, "You cannot help much if you don't have much." Or, "You cannot better others if you don't better yourself." It was when Joseph had become better that He could better the lives of his family members. It was when Esther had become better that she could be of help to her nation.

It is good to show concern. There is nothing wrong with that. However, do not let your concern for others prevent you from beginning and completing what will better you in life. Do not let concern derail you from completing...

Commitment

"Still another said, 'I will follow you, Lord; but first let
me go back and say goodbye to my family.' Jesus replied,
'No one who puts a hand to the plow and looks back is fit
for service in the kingdom of God.' " [vs. 61-62]

The third excuse of this man: **I cannot do without**...

The problem here is that this man was looking for an excuse not to follow Jesus. He wanted to keep his options open and be where he was interested. He undoubtedly liked Jesus. He would be a good Master, but he liked his family too. He is the distracted disciple who gets real excited and devoted for a while and then you do not see him for a while.

We can say that this man did not know what he wanted. He wanted Jesus and he wanted his family. He did not know what to choose in life. If you want to complete what you began in life you must be ready to make some choices that are dangerous, sacrificial, demanding, painful, hurtful, and risky. This guy still wants to kiss some people or please some people before he would take a step or make decision in his life. He wanted somebody to know about it. He wanted the clearance of somebody. He wanted the approval of somebody. Such people never begin or complete anything in life.

This man was only committed to what is convenient for him. If it is not convenient then it cannot be done. Listen, life is never convenient. Sometimes you don't feel like it, but you have to feel like it. This is commitment. If you want to succeed in your Christian life and journey as well as in your purpose in life, you must be committed to it. You must be committed to your dream, your ambition, your focus in life, your plan in life, and your goal in life. You must be committed to what is right.

This man wanted to be a convenient follower. Convenient followers are not followers at all because they will only accompany Jesus when it is convenient for their schedules. Jesus challenged him to set his priorities in place. So many people find it difficult to begin and complete something in life because of what they are committed or attached to in life. As a result, many have got stuck in the same place in life. Like this man, they have not detached from certain attachments in their lives. Many people are attached to things and people that will draw them back in life. Sometimes,

- Some are committed to gambling
- Some committed to an immoral life
- Some are committed to partying
- Some are committed to Face book
- Some are committed to the Internet
- Some are committed to watching movies
- Some are committed to doing nothing, but just sleeping
- Some are committed to talking, talking and talking

All these are distractions in life. What are you committed to in life? In life, your attachment will determine your accomplishment, and your commitment will determine your achievement. A person who is going nowhere in life can never show you how to get there in life. Who you listen to or hang out with in life will determine what you will end up with in life.

Let us hear what Jesus told the man, *"No one who puts a hand to the plow and looks back is fit for service in the kingdom of God."* The Message Bible says, *"Jesus said, 'No procrastination. No backward looks. You can't put God's kingdom off till tomorrow. Seize the day.' "*

The best thing that will help you excel and succeed in life is to make the right choices now. Don't put off what you are expected to begin. Don't put off your dreams because of somebody. Don't allow anyone to determine where you are going in life. Be ready to begin and be ready to finish what you began.

Sometimes, you have to make your life choices by yourself. For you to complete what you began life as well as to complete successfully in life, don't let people decide for you and don't let people choose for you. Don't choose someone above God in your life. Be committed to God and to what you want to do in life.

You must stay committed if you want to complete what you began in life. A farmer who is working on the plow must focus on what he is doing and not be looking here and there. He must not take his eyes off the line if he wants to complete well. Commitment is to be determined. It is to be resolute. It is to be unyielding. It is to be tenacious. It is to be sacrificial. It is to be focused. It is to be undaunted. It is refusing to give up. It is no retreat and no surrender. Commitment will make you complete.

You are to be committed to what you are doing if you want to complete excellently in life. There will be distractions. There will be noises. There will be discouragement. There will be criticism. There will be challenges. There will be opposition. But commitment will make you remain purposeful, powerful, and passionate for that thing which you have begun and which you want to complete.

God who created us has given us the power to complete whatever we began. He Himself completed what He began. He completed the work of creation as well as the work of redemption. We have His DNA in us. We have the inherent power to complete what we began. You can complete whatever you began in life. This is one of the marks of excellence, to complete what you began in life. I pray that the Lord will deliver you from every spirit of failure, incompleteness, procrastination, and mediocrity. Amen.

CHAPTER NINE

Know What to Do to Keep You Going in Life...

> *"The race of life is not run by imitation but by motivation."*
> *"Life is not about relaxation, but destination."*

The most important thing about life is not where we began or where we are; it is where we are going. Many people focus on the past, where they have been, and ruin their present. Some focus on the present, where they are, and forget their future. Only few focus on the future, where they are going in life. Life is a journey with destination. It is not a vacation; it is a destination. It is not a recreation, but a destination.

This chapter was written to help the readers to focus on where they are going in life and how to keep going in life. It has been proven and observed that many people lose the groove to keep on keeping on in life. After reaching a point, level, and position in life, many people fail to keep on improving on where they are. They become complacent, comfortable, rested, settled, and develop "arrival mentality." Many have ceased to aspire, desire, acquire, and even perspire. They see themselves as reaching the highest point of their life, the pinnacle of their life. Many people have ceased to do what got them to where they are in life in the first place. They have abandoned their first passion, vision, mission, motivation, and inspiration.

Apostle Paul, writing from the prison in the city of Philippi, was challenging his readers about what might be their wrong assumption about his mission in life. They have regarded him as their hero and model in life. They have regarded and canonized him as infallible, indefatigable, invulnerable, and immutable. To this, Paul said no. Paul saw life as a journey toward a destination. Paul saw life as a place where it is not over until it is over. Paul saw life as a continuum phase and not a momentum place. Paul saw life as a place where if you stop at any point, you will reach a diminishing return.

The focus of this chapter is to challenge you to keep on from where you are. To let you know that there is always a level better than where you are. This chapter is meant to motivate you to know that unless you keep going you cannot get there. Also to let you know that there is a destination that is better than any earthly or material destination which we have attained in life. There is a destination better than your present destination.

Many people struggle with how to maintain their success and excellence in life. We have people who were once successful and now unsuccessful; many who were once excellent but now un-excellent. The problem with success and excellence in life is this: *If you don't maintain it, you cannot retain it. If you don't improve it you cannot conserve it.* Therefore, how can you keep going to your ultimate and final destination in life without getting stuck at your present destination in life? From the reading of Philippians 3:12-14, the following are the steps you have to take.

Aspiration

*"Not that I have already obtained all this, or have
already arrived at my goal..."*[v. 12a]

Sometimes one can get stuck in the euphoria of the present achievement, success, and excellence, that one becomes overly egocentric, megalomania, and self-centered. One at this level can develop the, "I have conquered the whole world and there is nothing to conquer again," attitude. One can become self-conceited and act like Nebuchadnezzar in the Book of Daniel chapter 4 verse 30 who said: *"Look at this, Babylon the great! And I built it all by myself, a royal palace adequate to display my honor and glory!"* (The Message) Nebuchadnezzar developed the "I have arrived" mentality which has been the beginning of diminishing return in life. To say or think that you are there when you are not there will prevent you from getting there.

People regarded Apostle Paul to have gotten there or to have "obtained all this." At least his resume was impeccable and fantastic. He was from the tribe of Benjamin. He was a Hebrew to the core. He was a conservative and orthodox Jew. He was a Pharisee. He studied under Rabbi Gamaliel. He was a Roman citizen. He pioneered more churches than others. He wrote more epistles than others. He suffered more persecutions like flogging, shipwrecks, imprisonment, and court cases than others. Therefore, Paul had every course to be prideful because of his accomplishments. Paul did not have to aspire again. Paul did not have to try again. Paul did not have to keep on again. Paul did not have to pray more again. Paul did not have to read the Bible again. Paul did not have to evangelize again. Paul did not have to study again. Paul did not have to pioneer a church again. Paul had arrived! Don't you think the same way?

But Paul did not let the past and the present blind him of the future which is the real destination. Let me tell you this, the real is in the future and not in the past and present. The past is the surreal; the present is the ideal; and the future is the real. Therefore, don't mistake the past and present for the future. The past may look surreal, and the present look like ideal, but the future is the real. Therefore, it is dangerous to settle for the surreal (past), ideal (present) instead of the real (future).

This is what Paul did. That is why he said, *"Not that I have already obtained all this, or have already arrived at my goal."* This verse and the two following are full of allusions to the Grecian races. The word rendered "attained" signifies, to have arrived at the goal and won the prize, but without having as yet received it." (The Pictorial Bible) Furthermore, the word translated "goal" (NIV) or "perfect" (NKJV), is from the Greek word *teleos* which can mean moral or Christian perfection. However, this word is being used here in reference to the games that were celebrated in Greece, and to show that he had not completed his course and arrived at the goal, so as to receive the prize. Hence, this would mean that he had not yet received the crown which he aspired after as the result of his efforts in this life. Therefore, Paul was ready and willing to aspire.

This is the thesis of this point: ASPIRATION. Life is about aspiration and not expiration. Your destination would require aspiration. What is aspiration? It is desiring, longing, aiming, ambitioning, craving, and wanting. It is refusing to be satisfied, to be settled, to be complacent, and to be contented in the little... I mean complacent. It is to refuse to settle for status quo, the past and the present.

Sometimes many develop settle for the now and will not aspire for the next. They forget that there is always a best and better than the present. That is why people are researching in order to improve on the present. There is always the need for improvement in life. No wonder someone has said, *"The biggest room in the world is the room for improvement."* This is the whole essence of aspiration: improvement. There is a better way to do whatever you are doing. That is why you need to aspire to be better than where you are today.

I have seen and heard many Christians who claim, as well as think and even act, as if they have reached perfection. Have they read what Paul said in this verse that. "I don't mean to say that I have already achieved these things or that I have already reached perfection?" (New Living Translation) Maybe they are greater and holier than Paul. I don't think there is anyone on this Earth who can claim to have reached this level. It is an ongoing effort until you die. You have to keep on keeping on. There is no spiritual perfectionist as some people think they are. They are only suffering from what I call Spiritual Obsessive-Compulsive Disorder (SOCD).

There should be an urge for aspiration and improvement in every domain of our life. That is, there is need to aspire and improve physically, socially, psychologically, and spiritually.

Devotion

"But I press on to take hold of that for which
Christ Jesus took hold of me." [v. 12b]

Paul here decided to change his so-called arrival, holier than thou and perfectionistic attitudes to a proactively progressive one. With this new attitude he said, *"But I press on,..."* This is what I call devotion. The words *"but I press on"* can also be rendered as "but I follow after." That is, I pursue the object of my devotion by striving to obtain it. The prize was seen in the distance, and he diligently and devotionally sought to obtain it. There is a reference here to the Grecian races, and hence, the meaning would be, "I steadily pursue my course." Are you pressing on or are you pressing down? Are you pressing forward or pressing backward?

It takes an act of devotion to press on or follow after. Many people give up easily. They give up on their dreams, ambitions, pursuits, and desires. They have the emotion to do it, but there is no devotion. They have the wish to do it, but there is no will. What is devotion? It is an extraordinary dedication, commitment, consecration, strong attachment and affection to a course. It is to be committed to a covenant, pledge and vow to do something. It is not looking back. It is determination to reach a point or a destination. Devotion produces passion, sacrifice, determination, and a refusing to give up or quit.

Two out of the greatest spiritual diseases that Christians can have are spiritual anemia and spiritual amnesia: lack of spiritual fervor and ignorance of spiritual advancement. This is always caused by distortion of the mind. That is, thinking wrongly:

- Thinking that one is the best and better than others.
- Thinking too highly of oneself.
- Thinking of advancing in the spiritual than others (Spiritual megalomania).
- Thinking that your spiritual opinion is the best.

Unless you renew your thinking in all these areas and others, you will not press on, but will remain in stagnant thinking that you are the best.

I repeat again, life is not about where you are, but where you are going. You must keep a destination in view if you want to press on in life. Where are you heading? You must be able to provide an honest answer to this question. Where are you coming from and where are you heading to? Unless you have a destination in view, you cannot have devotion, but only emotion. Emotion makes you to fantasize, daydream, wish, procrastinate, and contemplate. Whereas, devotion makes you to pursue, go after, act, take steps, take risks; whereas you will be ready to go extra miles, endure, and keep on going. It is devotion that will keep you away from looking back at the past, focusing on the present, but pressing to the future.

Devotion makes you to do all that it takes to get there. When others are complaining, devotion keeps you completing. When you are devoted to where you are going in life, you will never be distracted by what goes on around you. Distraction will cause you diversion in life. Devotion will take you to your destination in life. You need devotion and not just emotion…

Concentration

"But one thing I do: Forgetting what is behind and
straining toward what is ahead." [v. 13]

Apostle Paul here is here using the metaphor of a footrace to ascertain that Christian life involves continual forgetting of *"what is behind"* and exerting of energy on what is ahead. Here is the major problem that hinders many people from advancing or progressing either in life or in the spiritual or Christian life: failure to release and forget the past. Forgetting the past did not indicate obliterating the memory of the past, but a conscious refusal to let them absorb or take our attention. That is, not allowing the memory of the past to consume our passion and hinder our spiritual progress. There is no one who does not have past things to deal with. The past can be…

- Past failures and mistakes
- Past achievements and accomplishments
- Past offences, wrongs and hurts
- Past accidents
- Past problems
- Past experiences and background

Sometimes we are shaped and made by our past. The past is always powerful. The past always has a grip on our present as well as future. Sometimes the past can be a terrible monster that terrorizes the present and the future. Dealing with the past would require a conscious effort. It requires concentration or focusing hard. You must be ready to deal with your past or your past will deal with you. Hence, to deal with your past will require effort, perspiration.

In fact the expression *"Forgetting what is behind"* is an allusion to the Grecian races. Anyone in this race who is running to get the prize would not stop to look behind him to see how much ground he had run over, or who among his competitors had fallen behind. Instead, he would keep his eye steadily on the prize, and strain every nerve that he might obtain it. Should in case his attention was diverted and distracted for any reason, it would hinder his flight, and might lead to losing the crown. Therefore, Paul said that he was looking onward to the prize by fixing his eye intently on it. Because it was the only object in his view; therefore, he would not allow his mind to be diverted from that by the contemplation of the past.

Since you have a destination in view that is better and greater than the past; therefore, release the past so that you can advance in life. Here is what the writer of Hebrews says in 12: *"Therefore, since we are surrounded by such a huge crowd of witnesses to the life of faith, let us strip off every weight that slows us down, especially the sin that so easily trips us up. And let us run with endurance the race God has set before us. ² We do this by keeping our eyes on Jesus, the champion who initiates and perfects our faith. Because of the joy awaiting him, he endured the cross, disregarding its shame." (New Living Translation)*

Because what is ahead is better than what is in the past and present, then you must be ready to do what Paul did. It is *"straining toward what is ahead."* The New Living Translation says, *"... looking forward to what lies ahead."* It is looking forward and not looking backward. It takes efforts to look forward when you are faced with the reality of the past and present. You have to look forward spiritually and psychologically. You need to look forward by faith even if you don't see anything ahead. Just keep going. Just keep focusing on Him. You don't have to know or see your destination before you will take steps to go there. Just look by faith and not by sight. There is something ahead of you… There is something ahead for you… Just make every effort to forget the past and look forward.

Destination

"I press on toward the goal to win the prize for which God
has called me heavenward in Christ Jesus." [v. 14]

Instead of focusing on the past, Apostle Paul changed his focus. He refocused on the ultimate goal for his life. Listen to him, *"I press on toward the goal to win the prize for which God has called me heavenward in Christ Jesus."* That is, he decided to focus on the major and not on the minor. He was ready to focus on the destination and not on the vacation. This world is like a vacation. It is for vocation and relaxation. The real destination is heaven. That is the best place. That is the real place. That is where we are going.

Dear reader, the goal of life and Christianity is not to be ordained or given a position in the church. It is not to occupy many ministries in the church. It is not to be a member of the most important mega church in the city. It is not to belong to a denomination. It is not to be married to a Christian spouse. It is not to buy and ride the best car. It is not to own and live in the best house. It is not to win the Grammy award. It is not material gain. It is to win the prize for which God has called us. What is this prize? The Contemporary Bible renders verse 14 in this way to describe the prize: *"I run toward the goal, so that I can win the prize of being called to heaven. This is the prize that God offers because of what Christ Jesus has done."* What is this prize? It is the crown which we shall receive during rapture.

Do you think that everything ends here? Not at all. Here is not the final place. Here is not the resting place. Here is not the destination. The only things you can receive here on Earth are remunerations, salaries, allowances, and awards. Only when you get to the final destination, in heaven, that you will get reward. Do you know that reward is greater than award? It is better to get reward in heaven than to get many awards on Earth. Does what you are doing on Earth qualify you for reward in heaven?

This is the prize and the goal of salvation. God did not save us to become a Bishop, Apostle, Reverend, Pastor, Elder, Evangelist, Revered Canon, Most Senior Apostle, and so on. He saved us so that we can be raptured and qualified for heaven. Listen to what Paul said again about this prize in 1 Cor. 9:27: *"No, I beat my body and make it my slave so that after I have preached to others, I myself will not be disqualified for the prize."* The prize is the goal of our salvation while the reward is the result of our service. The prize is the gateway to reward. If you don't make it to the rapture, then you cannot have any reward.

As you are about to finish the reading of this book, you need to check and assess yourself. I want you to honestly ask and answer these questions: Am I saved? Will I go to heaven if I die? Will I be rewarded in heaven for what I did here on Earth? Please I want you to know that it is not too late for you to accept Jesus Christ as your Lord and Savior. God bless you.

CHAPTER TEN

Maintain the Power of Hope

> *"When you lose hope you lose all."*

Hope is a powerful force in life. It is more powerful than faith. Many people exercise faith, but few people exercise hope. Hope is the feeling that what you are expecting, believing, and dreaming about will happen. It is refusal to give up and the ability to hold on. Although faith and hope are like brothers, but hope is greater than faith. However, the two are intertwined.

Webster dictionary has defined faith as "unquestioning belief, complete trust or confidence." Whereas, hope is defined as "a feeling that what is wanted will happen; desire accompanied by expectation." (www.merriam-webster.com/dictionary/hope).

When you look at the definitions of the two words, one is about conviction (faith) while the other is anticipation or expectation (hope). What does this mean? There is one thing for one to have faith, confidence, and trust in God for what He is going to do, but there is another thing to have anticipation or expectation towards its realization. You can have faith or conviction that you will become what God has created you to become in life, but you may lack hope or expectation to keep you believing.

Many people have started with faith or great conviction, but have lost the faith because they have become hopeless. They have lost hope in what they believe in. Here is the fact: it is possible to have faith and not have hope, or to have hope and not have faith. Hope is what helps us to achieve what we believe in. Hope is what keeps you going by faith. It is the motivation and inspiration for our faith. You can have faith in God and later lose hope in God. You can have faith in yourself and later lose hope in yourself. Faith and hope can be compared in the following ways:

- Faith is rooted in the knowing, that is, in a fact or what you know, but hope is based in the volition, in your will. You believe or have faith because you know…..that God will do it or it will happen. Whereas, you hope, not because you know, but because you will know.
- Faith focuses on the now or on the present promises of God and your dreams in life, but hope focuses on the future, an anticipation or expectation of their realization.
- Faith claims it…..but hope proclaim it. Faith says, "It is settled", hope says, "It will be settled."
- Faith gets you started, hope gets you going.
- Faith motivates you, hope inspires you.

The passage chosen for this chapter, Romans 4:18-22, describes the power of hope in the exercising of faith. Sometimes, you will get to the point in your life when you cannot hold on with faith again. You will get to the time when your faith is becoming weakened, shaken, and fallen. You will get to the point when believing in God does not make sense to you or when believing in yourself is impossible. Ask those who have been there, and they will tell you. I have been there. I did not know what to do again. The past, present and even the future looked very vague and foggy. I had lost the use of my two legs and arms. I was paralyzed and unable to move or do anything. The doctors said that they did not know what was wrong with me medically. The people of God prayed for me and were not sure whether I would be able to perform any activities of daily living (ADL) again. I lost my fine motor skills, ability to write and tie shoes and gross motor skills, ability to walk and kick. I became a necessary burden to everyone in my household. I lost faith in myself, in my future, and even in God. I thought that God had abandoned me. I thought that I would end up in life unfulfilled, unaccomplished, and irrelevant. But the power of hope kept me going. Hope helped me to see beyond who I was at that time, to who I would be in the future. Hope made me to believe that I could walk again. Sometimes when no one was around, I tried to stand and walk, but only to fall down. But hope kept me trying until I was able to walk again.

From our passage, we can carefully detect four things that hope does for faith. This shows that faith is not enough; hope must be included. Let us examine these four things which hope does for our faith. That is, what is the impact of anticipation or expectation (hope) on conviction or trust (faith)?

From this passage we can observe that it took Abraham and Sarah 25 years of waiting before Isaac was born. It took 25 years of waiting before they realized the promise and purpose of God for their lives. But what kept them waiting on God? It is called HOPE. Let us examine from our passage the Power of Hope from Romans 4:18-22

Hope Releases Your Faith

"Even when there was no reason for hope, Abraham
kept hoping—believing that he would become the father
of many nations. For God had said to him, 'That's how
many descendants you will have!' " [v. 18, NLT]

"Against hope Abraham believed in hope…" [v. 18, NET Bible]

[*For Abraham, human reason for*] *hope being gone, hoped
in faith that he should become the father of many nations,
as he had been promised…"* [v. 18, Amplified].

What do we see here? We see a perfect example and model of the power of hope in the life of Abraham. The story and life of Abraham fully described the dynamics of hope and faith. In him, we see faith and hope in action. Our text, Romans 4:18-22 gives us a recap of the role which hope played in the expression of Abraham's faith. We only know and see him as the Father of Faith rather than of hope. However, we need to understand the Old Testament context of the life of Abraham before we can see the role of hope in his faith. However, a review of the life of Abraham's hope and faith is found in Genesis chapters 12 to 21.

- In Genesis 12, God called him and told him to move away from his family and people. He was to go to another land which God would showed him. God gave him a promise that He would make him great. Abraham was 75 years old while Sarah was 65 at this time. He obeyed God, partially.
- In Genesis 15, Abraham complained to God that he has kept his own part of the bargain of the covenant or promise by leaving his people while God has not kept His own part, because He has not given him a child. And God reassured him that He would do all that He has promised.
- In Genesis 16, Sarah could not endure or wait for the time when God would fulfill all that He has promised. Out of desperation and frustration, she suggested another route or alternative solution to make the promise come to pass. Abraham obeyed and took the shortcut to fulfill and find the solution to the problem. He was 86 years old when Ishmael was born. Sarah was 76.

- In Genesis 17 and 18, the Lord reassured Abraham that his wife Sarah would give birth to the promised child despite their old age. Abraham objected and suggested to God that he was okay with Ishmael, the son of Hagar. But Sarah laughed and doubted God.

- In Genesis 21, God fulfilled His promise to Abraham and Sarah by giving them a child, Isaac. Abraham was 100 years old while Sarah was 90.

From the Old Testament and Genesis account of the life of Abraham, Paul developed the thesis of hope as a catalyst for faith. The story shows human nature and reality of the life of Saint Abraham. He is like any one of us. Sarah is like any one of us. As human beings, after many years, days, and months with no sign that God would do it, Abraham began to lose hope, trust and confidence in God. Even though he was worshiping and obeying God, but he was not happy inside him. He was angry at God inside, but laughing with people outside. In the Spirit he was contented with his situation, but in the body he was upset and frustrated. No wonder he agreed to the desperate move suggested by Mummy Sarah in Genesis 16 by agreeing to marry Hagar as the second wife and to sleep with her. Sometimes, *losing hope would make you to lose your morals.* You will compromise. You will want to do as others are doing it. How could he have agreed to do such a thing? What about you, are you going to do the same thing or what are you doing or have done when your faith has become weakened?

Abraham lost his faith in God and he said to Him in Genesis 17:17-18: "Then Abraham bowed down to the ground, but he laughed to himself in disbelief. *"How could I become a father at the age of 100?' he thought. 'And how can Sarah have a baby when she is ninety years old?' So Abraham said to God, 'May Ishmael live under your special blessing!'* " [NIV] We can hear Abraham telling God this: "Let me leave with what I am rather than what you promised that you would do. That is, "I don't know if you are going to do it, but I am okay with what I have done to solve my problem. The Ishmael that I have is better than Isaac that I have not had. Let me settle with whosoever comes my way, whatever comes my way, anything that comes. I don't care again God." Sometimes, many of us settle for what works now and not what will work in the future. We only have faith in God when or if He can do it now.

But in Genesis 18:11-14 God specifically and directly informed him and Sarah that they would have a child. Not in a vision, or through a dream, or by a prophet, but directly and personally. But Sarah did not want to hear this again. Hear what the Bible says,

> ¹⁰" *[The Lord] said,' I will surely return to you when the season comes round, and behold, Sarah your wife will have a son.' And Sarah was listening and heard it at the tent door which was behind Him.*

> ¹¹ *Now Abraham and Sarah were old, well advanced in years; it had ceased to be with Sarah as with [young] women. [She was past the age of childbearing].*

> ¹² *Therefore Sarah laughed to herself, saying, After I have become aged shall I have pleasure and delight, my lord (husband), being old also?*

> ¹³ *And the Lord asked Abraham, Why did Sarah laugh, saying, Shall I really bear a child when I am so old?*

> ¹⁴ *Is anything too hard or too wonderful for the Lord? At the appointed time, when the season [for her delivery] comes around, I will return to you and Sarah shall have borne a son.*" [Amplified]

Please don't blame Sarah. She has had enough. She had been seeing women becoming pregnant and giving birth. She had attended and gave gifts at baby showers. She had waited and believed every year that her own time would come. But now she was about 90 years old and had reached the postmenopausal stage of life. Her faith had resigned to fate. *It is when your faith fails or is failing that hope is needed.* Hope will keep your faith going. Even though Sarah could not believe again, but the faith of Abraham was activated and released. This is what Romans 4:18 is saying. It says, *"Even when there was no reason for hope, Abraham kept hoping—believing that he would become the father of many nations. For God had said to him, 'That's how many descendants you will have.' "*

The hope that was against him was natural hope. This is hope that is based on reality or what you can see. For Abraham and Sarah, all the possibilities, circumstances, and conditions which predicate hope were against them. All circumstances were against their hope in having a child. Looking at themselves, all they could see was infertility, impossibility, impotence, and menopause. What do you see when you look at yourself or at your situation? Sometimes you will see dead-end, roadblocks, failure, mediocrity, stagnation, and stagnation. But, against all to the contrary, Abraham believed. How? He believed in hope based on God's all-sufficiency. That God is sufficient to do whatever looks insufficient in his life. That God could make him to become the father of many nations.

This verse says that even though there was no reason to hope in what God said He would do, Abraham continued to hope. He did not allow his condition to kill his expectation. *Your expectation should be greater than your situation. Don't give up your expectation… your hope. Don't give up. Refuse to give up because God has not given up on your case.* It does not matter how long you have been waiting or will continue to wait… keep hoping. Even if it looks as if there is no point or reason to believe that God will do it again…keep on hoping. Even if you say my faith cannot take it again… keep on hoping. Hebrews 10:23 says, *"Let us hold tightly without wavering to the hope we affirm, for God can be trusted to keep his promise."* [NLT]

You have not come to the end of the road because when a road closes on you another road will open for you. Hope will keep you going even when you don't feel like going on again. Hope will help you to release your faith. Hebrews 11:1 says:

"Now faith is confidence in what we hope for and assurance about what we do not see." (NIV)

"Faith is the confidence that what we hope for will actually happen; it gives us assurance about things we cannot see." (New Living Translation)

"Now faith is the assurance (the confirmation, the title deed) of the things [we] hope for, being the proof of things [we] do not see and the conviction of their reality [faith perceiving as real fact what is not revealed to the senses]." (Amplified)

Faith is what is taking place right now. Hope is something that we expect to happen in the future. By faith you believe in the truth of the word; whereas by hope you wait for the fulfilling of it. Faith makes you to look at what God has promised you, while hope makes you wait on what He has promised you. Faith is the check for money while hope is the money. Faith is the fact that God will do it. Hope is the expectation and realization of what God said He would do. Hope keeps you believing. Hope helps you to be patient in waiting for the manifestation of your expectation. Hebrews 6:15 has this to say about Abraham: *"Then Abraham waited patiently, and he received what God had promised."* [v.15] Don't give up your faith in what He said would do in your life. Don't overrun yourself. Don't envy others. Don't compete with others. Don't settle for now. Have hope in what is coming.

Believe it and hope in it. This hope is the anchor for your soul, according to Hebrews 6:19-20:

> *"This hope we have as an anchor of the soul, both sure and steadfast, and which enters the Presence behind the veil,* [20] *where the forerunner has entered for us, even Jesus, having become High Priest forever according to the order of Melchizedek."* [NKJV]

> *"This hope is a strong and trustworthy anchor for our souls. It leads us through the curtain into God's inner sanctuary.* [20] *Jesus has already gone in there for us. He has become our eternal High Priest in the order of Melchizedek."* [Vs. 19-20]

Jesus Christ is the object and ground of the believer's hope, and so it is a steadfast hope. We need to fix or anchor our hope on Him and not on any other thing. Hope helps you to release your faith in Jesus Christ. That is why, hope is not based on WHAT you are expecting but WHO you are expecting. Hope is not based on WHAT you want but WHO you want. Hope is not based on the PROBLEM, but on the PERSON. Hope is not based on WHERE you are but, WHERE you will be. Hope is not based on the SEEN, but on the UNSEEN. Hope releases the power of faith in God and in Jesus Christ and not in the problem.

Hope Maximizes Your Faith

> *"Without weakening in his faith, he faced the fact that his body was as good as dead—since he was about a hundred years old—and that Sarah's womb was also dead."* [v. 19, NIV]

"And Abraham's faith did not weaken, even though, at
about 100 years of age, he figured his body was as good
as dead—and so was Sarah's womb." [v. 19, NLT]

Another power of hope is that it maximizes the potential and capacity of faith. One thing is to have faith in God and that He would do whatever He has promised. It is another thing for faith to be increased and able to withstand challenges. This is what is called the living faith. It is a faith that does not waiver. It is a faith that does not become weak. It is a faith that does not become sick or weak. Hope is like a booster that enhances the full capacity of faith. The capacity of faith is called the measure of faith. Everybody's faith has a capacity, a measure. Your measure of faith will determine your measure of coping. Your measure of faith will determine how long and how well you will hold under pressures, challenges, disappointments, and setbacks. But hope helps in maximizing or increasing the measure of faith. Hope develops your faith. Hope adds more value to your faith.

Sometimes in life, some things will happen that will challenge our faith. It is easy to say, "I have faith," but it is difficult to determine the level or capacity of that faith. You cannot claim that you have faith, not until that faith has been tried and tested. It is easy to brag or say, "I am a winner," but how many wars have you fought? *It is hope that maximizes the capacity of faith.* Sometimes your faith will be under fire and attack. When faith says, "I cannot take it again," hope says, "It is well for my soul."

Faith is based on fact. That is why Hebrews 11:1 defines it as the, "... assurance of things hoped for." Faith is the assurance of what you are hoping. It is the assurance that God will do it. Assurance is based on fact. It is based on the fact of God's promise. *But what happens when it seems that the promise is no more certain due to certain circumstances?* That is what Romans 4:19 is saying. It says that Abraham was faced with the fact that *his body was as good as dead—and so was Sarah's womb.*

In other words, when the means by which God will do it have become damaged or meaningless, what should we do? God said that he would bless me, but now I have lost my job. God said that I will succeed in my academics, but now I am failing this course and repeating this class. God said that I will not die, but live, but the doctors have just diagnosed me with a terrible disease. God said that He will bless me, but now my present income is not even enough. God said that what He has joined together, let no one put asunder, but now my marriage is falling apart. This is when reality is confronting our faith in God. This is when you say, "Based on what has happened to me or my present condition, I don't think that God can do it again." What happens when what you are experiencing is greater than what you are expecting?

But listen to what the beginning of Romans 4:19 says, *"And Abraham's faith did not weaken."* When Abraham got to that period in his life, his faith did not weaken. Maybe your faith is becoming weakened. Maybe your faith is becoming discouraged. Maybe your faith is becoming depressed. Maybe your faith is tired. You have to do what Abraham did. What did Abraham do? He exercised hope. Listen to what the first line of verse 19 says again: *"Without weakening in his faith…."* What does it mean? He did not allow his faith to become weak by exercising the power of hope. He began to see himself as God has called him or said he was – father of many nations. He began to act as if it has happened. Hope makes you to begin to act as if it has happened. Hope makes you to act abnormal, unusual, and extraordinary. You have to change your attitude about your condition. Don't let your hope die. You need hope to survive what your faith cannot survive. You need hope to add more oil to maximize the function of your faith. Sometimes your faith can become dysfunctional and malfunctioned. You need hope to increase the potential of your faith. The book of Isaiah 40:31 says: *"But those who hope in the Lord will renew their strength. They will soar on wings like eagles; they will run and not grow weary, they will walk and not be faint."* Hope gives you wings to soar on, even when the storms are trying to pull you down. Another version of Bible says, *"Those who wait..."* [KJV] Faith is believing that it will happen. Hope is waiting for it to happen. That is why you have to wait for your sun to come out, don't force it. Someone says, *"Hope is to be expectant when everything seems hopeless."* *"When the world says "give up," hope says, "Try one more time."* Faith is the gas or fuel that gives power to the car, but hope is the engine oil that keeps the engine run smoothly.

Hope Strengthens Your Faith

"Yet he did not waver through unbelief regarding the promise of God, but was strengthened in his faith and gave glory to God." [v. 20, NIV]

"Abraham never wavered in believing God's promise. In fact, his faith grew stronger, and in this he brought glory to God." [v. 20, NLT]

The Contemporary English Version Bible describes what it means to wavier in the following words: *"But Abraham never doubted or questioned God's promise."* Hence, to waiver means to doubt. To doubt means to be in the state of unbelief. It is not trusting God again that He can do it. Doubt is developing lack of trust in God. Doubt makes you seek for an alternative solution. Doubt makes you put your hope in someone or something else. Doubt makes you lose hope. Doubt makes you become unstable in your faith or stance with God. Even though Abraham wavered once, but he became more steady and steadfast with God. He refused to allow his problem to determine his action.

Like Abraham, sometimes doubt will make you to doubt yourself and also to doubt God. But later, Abraham removed his focus from himself or Sarah, but put his focus on God. Abraham refused to believe what his senses were telling him about his condition. He refused to accept what his feelings were telling him about his situation. Sometimes, *it does not make sense to hope... but there is a sense in hope. A hopeless person is a senseless person.* When faith says, "I cannot take this any longer," hope says, "I know I can do all things through Jesus Christ who strengthens me."

The faith of Abraham grew stronger because it was strengthened by hope through praise. He was praising God for what he has not received from God. The Bible says that, *"Abraham never wavered in believing God's promise. In fact, his faith grew stronger, and in this he brought glory to God." [NLT]"* Wow! The Bible says that his faith grew stronger. How did he do it? He did not allow his problem to break him, but only to make him. He did not allow his problem to overcome him, but only to make him an overcomer. He did not allow his problem to define and describe who he was. He did not allow his problem to truncate his focus and purpose.

Many people magnify their problems more than God. In other words, they have more faith in their problems more than in God. They can tell you how long they have been in the problem and how serious the problem has been. However, they cannot tell you how powerful God is in their life or how hopeful they are in spite of the problem. Sometimes, the problem is not the problem, but the problem is how we respond to the problem. Abraham did not allow his problem to become his undertaker, but only his teacher. His problem helped him to draw closer and nearer to God. The Bible says that, *"...but was strengthened in his faith and gave glory to God."* How can you give glory to God in problem? It is when you have hope in the Lord that He can bring out the best out of the problem.

This is what strengthened his faith the more. He began to give God adoration even in the midst of his humiliation. He did not do what many of us are doing: giving glory to God only for appreciation. Instead, he gave glory to God in expectation and anticipation. This is the power of hope in action. Hope adds more power to his faith. It makes his faith powerful. Hope turns faith to "worshiping faith" instead of "begging faith." Hope turns complacent faith to excellent faith. Do you give glory to God for what He has done for you or for what He has not done for you? Hope sees beyond what has not happened to what will happen, from what has not to what will be.

Hope Stabilizes Your Faith

[21] "being fully persuaded that God had power to do what he had promised. [22] This is why it was credited to him as righteousness." [vs. 21-22, NIV]

"Fully satisfied and assured that God was able and mighty to keep His word and to do what He had promised.[22] That is why his faith was credited to him as righteousness (right standing with God)." [vs. 21-22, Amplified]

The last power of hope is that it stabilizes your faith. It helps you to maintain your balance and stand with God. It helps you to stay firm and steadfast in the Lord. Hope helps you to hold on in faith. Even though Abraham had not seen the fulfillment of God's promise, but he held on by faith. Even though he did not know when and how it will happen, but he held on by faith. His hope helped him to hold on by faith. To stabilize means to be stable, to be firmed, to be steady, and to be unmoved.

One of the things that happen when in crisis and trouble or when faced with challenges of life is to panic. From panic to worry, from worry to anxiety, from anxiety to doubt, and from doubt to instability, many thoughts will come to your mind. Many decisions will come to your mind also. You will not be sure of what to do. You will be confused, distressed, and depressed.

You will lose your appetite for doing anything, for prayer, for going to church, for sleeping, for eating, and for fellowship with God. This is when you give up on God. This is when faith in God crashes. This was the moment when Job's wife told him to curse God, to denounce God, and to abandon God. This was the time when Sarah told Abraham to marry and sleep with Hagar. This is the moment of compromise. This is when we compromise our faith under the guise of "God will understand." This is when we need hope.

How did Abraham display his hope? Verse 21 says, "...*being fully persuaded that God had power to do what he had promised.*" What or who persuaded him? It is the person of God. He was persuaded by who God was to him. He knew that God was reliable and dependable. He knew God to be the creator, all powerful, all knowing, all sufficient, inexhaustible, eternal, everlasting, immutable, great provider, greater than the greatest, better than the best, Almighty, ancient of days, the Lord God of all flesh, the Mighty One, and so on. The phrase *"being fully persuaded"* means to be thoroughly, properly and absolutely convinced. The Greek word used here is plērophorētheis (πληροφορηθεὶς) meaning to be fully assured. Abraham was fully assured of the faithfulness of God even in the midst of his unfaithfulness. Hope helped him to hold on in faith and onto the faithfulness of God. This stabilized his faith from wandering.

Sometimes you need to encourage yourself with the faithfulness of God. You need to persuade yourself to hold on to God. You need to speak hope to yourself. You need to assure yourself that *God was able and mighty to keep His word and to do what He had promised.* [Amplified] You need to hold on to God. You need hope in God and not in what you are expecting from God. You need to focus on Him and not the things you are expecting. You need to stop seeing God as an ATM machine which you use as a drive through to get what you want. You have to see God as He is and not only for what He does. You need to cultivate genuine relationship with God and not a consumer or economic relationship with Him. The type of faith you have in God will determine the type of relationship you will have with God. Do you have hope in God or hope in what you are expecting from God?

For Abraham, his hope was in God and this stabilized his faith in God. This was credited to him as righteousness because he held on to God. He continued to maintain his relationship with God. Righteousness is being in right relationship with God. *He did not allow what God has done or has not done to determine his relationship with God.* He did not base the tone and mode of his relationship with God with what is expecting from God. He did not bargain with God as many of us do. He did not give God any condition as many of us are doing. What about you? What determines your relationship with God? Is it what you have or what you don't have? Abraham's hope was not based on the birth of Isaac, but on the Lord of Isaac. It is not on the provision, but the Provider. His hope was on eternal God and not a material god. His hope transcended his expectation. His hope transcended the material and physical. *He valued his relationship with God more than his expectation from God.* His hope was not based on what God will do, but who God was. He did not view God from a consumer or economic or utilitarian perspective, but rather from a relational viewpoint. His faith was stabilized.

Only the power of hope can stabilize your faith. Your faith must be holistic. It must involve your mind, soul, body, and spirit. Your spirit cannot have faith while your body does not. Your spirit cannot have faith while your mind or soul is doubting. You need hope to stabilize your faith. You need hope to be fully assured and convinced that God is always faithful and reliable. It is not when He does it alone that makes Him faithful, but even when He does not do it. The faithfulness of God is not in what He does, it is in who He is.

President Barack Obama once said this about hope: *"Hope is that stubborn thing inside us that insists that something better awaits us so long as we have the courage to keep reaching, to keep working, and to keep fighting."*

But what if the Lord has not or does not do it? What happens to your hope? Must you feel discouraged or disappointed in God? The answer is NO. You have to move from earthly, physical, and material hope to heavenly or eternal hope. Hear what Hebrews 11:13-16:

> *13 "All these people were still living by faith when they died. They did not receive the things promised; they only saw them and welcomed them from a distance, admitting that they were foreigners and strangers on earth. 14 People who say such things show that they are looking for a country of their own. 15 If they had been thinking of the country they had left, they would have had opportunity to return. 16 Instead, they were longing for a better country—a heavenly one. Therefore God is not ashamed to be called their God, for he has prepared a city for them."* [NIV]

Verses 39-40 add the following:

> *39 "All these people earned a good reputation because of their faith, yet none of them received all that God had promised. 40 For God had something better in mind for us, so that they would not reach perfection without us."* [NIV]

Jesus is the ultimate hope of all believers. It is not the material things, but eternal life through Jesus Christ. This is our hope. This is the excellent hope. This is the greatest excellence anyone can attain. You may not have everything here, but you have everything there. No wonder Paul said: *"If we who are [abiding] in Christ have hope only in this life and that is all, then we are of all people most miserable and to be pitied."* [1 Corinthians 15:19, Amplified] May I tell you this before I close: *"Faith is not the belief that God will do what you want. It is the belief that God will do what is right."* (Max Lucado).

CHAPTER ELEVEN

Operate in the Power of Eagles

"It is the Power of God that Empowers the Power that is in you."

W e were created by power. We are sustained by power. We
must operate in power. The power of the Holy Spirit is
the greatest power in life. There is chemical power, solar power,
hydro-power, electric power, petroleum power, locomotive power,
economic power, political power, and so on. Without power, life
is useless. The Merriam-Webster Dictionary has defined power
as: "ability to act or produce an effect... ability to get extra-base
hits... capacity for being acted upon or undergoing an effect."
(http://www.merriam-webster.com/dictionary/power) It has
further been defined by another dictionary as: "ability to do or
act; capability of doing or accomplishing something... great or
marked ability to do or act; strength; might; force... the ability to
perform work." (http://dictionary.reference.com/browse/power)

Power is one of the integral parts of humans. Everything in
life is regulated and sustained by power. Everything is as the
result of power. It is like the cause behind every effect. In physics,
"power is the rate of doing work. It is equivalent to an amount of

energy consumed per unit time." (http://en.wikipedia.org/wiki/ Power_(physics) However, there is difference between power and energy. According to Prabhat (2011), "energy is the ability to do work, power is its measurement, which calculates the time by which the energy has been used. Energy is what one delivers and Power is the rate at which it is delivered." (http://www. differencebetween.net/science/difference-between-energy-and-power/) In order words, energy is the capability to do something while power is the rate at which it is being done.

The Lord has created us with the ability, capability, capacity, and velocity to do and become what He has created us for in life. That is why in Isaiah 40:29-31, the prophet, based on the metaphor and imagery of eagles, describes how we are empowered and powered up by God. In verse 28, the prophet describes God as omnipotent and omniscience. Hence, based on His omnipotence, He has created us with potency. In other words, the Lord did not create us to be impotent (not just biological or reproductive), but to be potent. He did not create us to be invalid (not just physiological), but to be valid. The power for potency was first bequeathed into the first man, Adam, when God breathed into his nostril and though him transferred or imputed to all human beings. Therefore, this power and energy that is in us can be said to be potential (stored), kinetic (motioned), and mechanical (active). This divine given power and energy is the sine qua non for our excellence, success, accomplishment, and achievement in life.

Isaiah equates the power of God that is in us with the power of eagles. Eagles are one of the most powerful of all the birds. Eagles symbolize strength, power, and might. From this text, we want to examine six powers or energies which the eagles have and which make them to be champions and excellent amongst other birds and which are necessary in our lives to make us realize, actualize, and maximize all the potencies which the omnipotent God has imputed into us. What are these powers?

Before we begin to examine these six powers, let me tell you this: Any other power will not carry you far in life, only the power of God will. Any other power is temporal, ephemeral, and limited; only the power of God in you is permanent, lasting, and will last. Here are the six powers as inferred from Isaiah 40:31.

Waiting

"But those who wait on the Lord... " (NKJV)

One of the powers that eagles possess is the ability to wait. By waiting I mean patience. An eagle does not rush and struggle to be an eagle in a day. An eagle does not begin to fly or soar in a day. She must first wait. She must wait until she is processed and made. The baby eagle must first learn and be modeled by the mother eagle. She must learn to submit and hide under the wings of the mother eagle. She must wait until she has been mentored, tutored, and trained to fly. Even though she has the innate and inner power to fly, but must wait for the outer power to develop her. Life is not about knowing how to, it is also about learning how to. In Psalms 130:5-6, David said: *"I wait for the Lord, my soul waits, And in His word I do hope. My soul waits for the Lord More than those who watch for the morning—Yes, more than those who watch for the morning."* There is power in waiting.

The waiting time for eagles is for preparation before manifestation. This is the time when the baby eagle learns how to fly. The baby eagle during this time is like any ordinary bird. She is treated and looked at as a chicken. But she continues to patiently wait. The waiting period is a horrible period. She must graduate from the school of waiting before moving to the next level in her life. No wonder Job 23:10 said, *"But He knows the way that I take; When He has tested me, I shall come forth as gold."* The waiting time is the testing time. This is the period of character development. This is the time to develop patience, endurance, determination, commitment, focus, sacrifice, and seriousness of the baby eagle.

Everybody needs this power, the power of waiting. People want to win, but they are not ready to wait. People want to achieve and succeed, but they are not willing to wait. People look for a shortcut to the destination, drive through to the solution, and emergency approach to the problem. Nobody wants to stay on the waiting list and waiting line of life. Everybody is in rush to get there and to make it. Nobody wants to wait for anything. Our generation has become a rushing generation. There is no more speed limit of life. This generation is not ready to observe and obey the speed limit of life. Everyone is guilty of violating the traffic regulation of life. Our generation does not want to wait for the light to turn green again before they cross. Everyone is now rushing and ignoring the yellow and red light of life; they have no more patience to wait.

We are living in an age of fast and the fast lane. The assumption is that the fastest is the best, and the quickest is the best. Hence, this quickest, fastest, and speediest mentality has made us to settle for quantity instead of quality, magic instead of miracle, solution instead of answer, cure instead of healing, and inefficiency instead of efficiency. Furthermore, we are now settling for the utilitarianism, the benefits of actions, and situationism, motives behind actions. Hence, the popular axiom has been, "the means justifies the end" or "the end justifies the end." The power or spirit of waiting is now missing in the daycare, in the kindergarten, in the primary, in the junior high, in the senior high, in the college, in business, in the pastoral ministry, in premarital relationships, in marital relationships, in family relationships, in friendships, and so on.

Dear readers, we are wired by God to wait. God has wired us with two autonomic nervous systems in the brain, which are called sympathetic and parasympathetic. These two act together to sustain the body's homeostatic state. The purpose of the sympathetic nervous system (SNS) is to activate the response of the body during stressful situations. On the other hand, parasympathetic nervous system (PNS) helps in conserving functions when the body is at rest. In other words, PNS helps in restoring the organism to its normal position of rest or waiting. It is in waiting that we derive our strength. There is power in waiting. Eagles know how to wait. Human beings do not know how to wait. We do not like to wait for God's time. We do not like to wait for God's will. We do not know how to wait for God's promise. We do not know how to wait for God's purpose. Waiting is considered a wasting of time. That was why Sarah could not wait. She suggested and rushed her husband, Abraham, to sleep with her maid so that she could bear him a son. Abraham agreed because he was tired of waiting. But God would not substitute their solution for His answer. They must wait for Isaac. Their inability to wait produced Ishmael, meaning God hears; whereas their waiting produced Isaac, which means God makes me laugh. Which one do you want to settle for? Ishmael (God hears) or Isaac (God makes me laugh)? Waiting would make you laugh at last in life, but rushing would make you cry or regret in life. Desperation is always the father of frustration.

You must learn to wait. Don't jump the queue. Waiting does mean that you are passive, inactive, complacent, indolent, and docile. Waiting is hoping, trusting, believing, and focusing on God. I love the way James describes this waiting in James 5:7-8: *"Therefore be patient, brethren, until the coming of the Lord. See how the farmer waits for the precious fruit of the earth, waiting patiently for it until it receives the early and latter rain... You also be patient. Establish your hearts, for the coming of the Lord is at hand."* (NKJV) Here is how the Message Bible puts it: *"Meanwhile, friends, wait patiently for the Master's Arrival. You see farmers do this all the time, waiting for their valuable crops to mature, patiently letting the rain do its slow but sure work. Be patient like that. Stay steady and strong. The Master could arrive at any time."*

From these two verses, you would see that the farmers do not wait on nothing. They were waiting on what they have done or what they have planted. They have already sown, invested, planted, and committed to something. They were only waiting on God to bring harvest. They have to wait for the result to come. They cannot force the seeds planted to grow. They must wait. As they are waiting, they must continue to keep the farm and clear the weeds. This shows that you cannot be waiting on nothing, you must be waiting on something. What are you waiting for? How long have you been waiting? Keep on waiting. You cannot be great in anything unless you know how to wait. Nobody begins at the top and lasts. Jesus waited for 30 years for the ministry of three and half years. Moses waited for 80 years for the ministry of 40 years. Eagles do not begin to fly in the air, but on the ground. You can never be on the mountaintop unless you know how to wait in the valley.

Renewing

"Shall renew their strength..." (NKJV)

Renewing is another power of eagles. The strength of eagles is in renewal. To renew means to rejuvenate, to repair, to reinvigorate, to re-empower, to reinforce, to re-energize and to recharge. The eagle knows when to discharge and later recharge. The eagles are regarded as champions among other birds because they know how to retreat and renew. They have the power of renewal. This usually occurs in what is called the "molting process." This is the wilderness time in the life of eagles. After living for some years, like say 30, eagles begin to lose their feathers and their claws and begin to act as turkeys or chickens. During this time, eagles lose the ability to fly, to see, and to eat. The eagles going through molting gather at a mountain place and wait on the rays

139

of the sun to shine on them. The other or older eagles who have gone through this process and who are soaring would come and drop food for them to eat and survive. They will continue to stay and wait there until they are renewed with all their feathers and claws grown back. Then they will soar and catch up with other eagles in the sky.

The Hebrew word translated "renew" here means to change, to revive, and to make to flourish again. This idea is what Job has in mind in Job 14:7-9 when he said, *"For there is hope for a tree if it is cut down, that it will sprout again and that the tender shoots of it will not cease. [But there is no such hope for man.] Though its roots grow old in the earth and its stock dies in the ground, Yet through the scent [and breathing] of water [the stump of the tree] will bud and bring forth boughs like a young plant."* (Amplified Bible). The idea of the power of renewal is that there comes a time in life when one needs to be refreshed, renewed, revived and rejuvenated emotionally, psychologically, spiritually, physically, martially, and financially.

What makes eagles to be stronger and respected than other birds is their power of renewal. They know that sometimes they become depreciated, obsolete, irrelevant, devalued, and moribund. But they know how to renew. Many people do not understand the language of renewal or change. They are conservative, orthodoxy, traditional and dogmatic in their approach to life. They don't believe in change, in new adventure, and trying a new thing. They are not renewed psychologically, emotionally, spiritually, and physically. They have forgotten that failure to renew is planning to fail in life. Life is not just being a hero or a superstar or winning always, but it is also about losing and failing. In spite of this, we must always remember the words of Winston Churchill that says, "Success is not final, failure is not fatal: it is the courage to continue that counts." Therefore, in life, failure is not final and final is not failure. You are never a failure until you have given up on yourself. The eagles during the molting stage do not give up on themselves. Like Job 14:7-9, they believe that there is still a hope for a tree when it is cut down. It can sprout again. It can flourish again. It can produce again.

To somebody reading this chapter, I want to inform you that there is a hope for you. There is a hope for your future even though you have lost hope in your past and present. You may be down to nothing now; there is hope. You may be down financially; there is hope for you. You may be down spiritually; there is a hope for you. You may be down emotionally; there is hope for you. A change is coming your way. You may be losing or have lost some feathers and claws now, but I want to tell you that there is hope for you and a change is on the way. God may be preparing or renewing you for greater heights. Just make sure that you abide under His shadow. You must submit to Him to renew you. God uses different and many things to repair, renew, rejuvenate, and refurbish us. Let God trim you. Let God work on you. Let God work on your purpose. Let God work on whatever that is decayed in your life. Don't trash your life; there is treasure in it. There is power of renewal in you, activate it and put it to action. You are only going through renewal or molting. The Lord is renewing. You are coming back stronger than before. Maybe the Lord wants you say like Job in Job 23:10 that, *"But He knows the way that I take; When He has tested me, I shall come forth as gold."* (NKJV) *" But He knows the way that I take [He has concern for it, appreciates, and pays attention to it]. When He has tried me, I shall come forth as refined gold [pure and luminous]."* (Amplified)

Soaring

"They shall mount up with wings like eagles…"

The Amplified Bible renders it in the following words: *"They will soar on wings;" "They shall lift their wings and mount up."* Based on the Hebrew translation, this phrase is translated as

141

"they shall ascend on wings as eagles," or "they shall lift up the wings as eagles." In Barnes' Notes, the Septuagint (The Greek translation of the Old Testament) translates it as, "They shall put forth fresh feathers (πτεροφυῄσουσιν *pterophuēsousin*) like eagles." (http://biblehub.com/commentaries/barnes/isaiah/40.htm) This imagery is based on the fact that the eagles always fly and rise on the most vigorous wing of any bird, and get to the altitude that is closer toward the sun. This, therefore, suggests strength, power, determination, purpose, and aiming high. These are what eagles do. They are birds of strength, power, determination, purpose, and mostly aiming high.

Eagles do not settle for the less; they aim high. They do not settle for the good and better; they aim for the best. They have attitude to higher altitude. Eagles do not just fly with their wings, but they soar or mount up in winds. When other birds are afraid of the winds, eagles make use of the winds. Their renewed wings always make use of the winds to fly higher than any other birds. In fact, they do not fly but they soar or mount up. What is the meaning of this? It means that eagles do not struggle with other birds to fly; they soar or mount up. Their wings are the potentials and abilities which God has given to them to soar and excel than other birds. When other birds hide their wings, eagles soar of fly with theirs.

Eagles do not just fly, but they soar. The word "soar" has a very motivational and inspirational meaning. It means, "To rise, fly, or glide high and with little apparent effort. To climb swiftly or powerfully. To glide in an aircraft while maintaining altitude. To ascend suddenly above the normal or usual level." (http://www.answers.com/topic/soar) Wow! What a great word! Research has shown that the bald eagles can fly to an altitude of 10,000 feet.

God has created and made us like eagles. He has designed us with potentials that will place us above and ahead as well as abilities to soar. However, sometimes, situations of life always make us think that we are limited, we are irrelevant, we are trashed, and we are nonentities. Believing all these false signals usually affects or influences our attitudes and in turn hampers our altitudes. In other words, we allow what we are to determine who we are. The "what" we are is our makeup vis-à-vis nature and nurture, but the "who" we are is what God has deposited in us. Sometimes we don't see who we are, but only see what we are. We always base our dreams, purposes and plans in life on what we are rather on who we are. Who we are is greater than what we are. What we are is how the world and men define us, but who we are is how the Word and God defines us.

The eagles may look ugly, hopeless, disappointed, discouraged, messy, helpless, failed, insignificant, and irrelevant during their molting stage, when all their feathers fall off. The other birds may look down on them, ridicule them, laugh at them, deride them, and mock them. But the eagles know that is not who they are. They know that what they look like is not who they are. Can you relate to this? Do you know that things may look rough and tough for you now and make you look down on yourself now? Somebody that is reading this book is going to bounce back from every set back in Jesus' name. Amen. But I have good news for you, *that is not who you are*. Don't let what you are stop you from becoming who you are. There is power for soaring, mounting and flying in you.

Your present financial, social, spiritual, marital, and relational feathers might have fallen that it looks as if you cannot soar again. Don't worry. You are made to soar and mount up and not to crawl. Your present crawling state is a practice toward your soaring. Your struggling is an inspiration for your soaring. Your present struggle is God's training ground for your soaring. Your present adversity is God's university for your prosperity. No wonder someone said, "My setbacks may have amused you, but my come backs are going to confuse you."

Remember that eagles rely on the wind and not just on their wings to fly higher than any other birds. Your wings (human might) will only take you a few altitudes or miles before you become faint and tired. But it is only the wind of God's power that will carry you through. Hear the Word of God: *"Then he said to me, 'This is what the Lord says to Zerubbabel: It is not by force nor by strength, but by my Spirit, says the Lord of Heaven's Armies.' "* (Zechariah 4:6, New Living Translation)

Speeding

"They shall run and not be weary..." (NKJV)

Eagles are known to run the fastest because they run with high speed. The following facts have been revealed about the speed of golden eagles:

- Average Horizontal Speed: 45–51 kilometer per hour or 28-32 miles per hour.
- Maximum Horizontal Speed: 129 kilometer per hour or 80 miles per hour.
- Average Diving Speed: 241 kilometer per hour or 150 miles per hour.
- Maximum Air Speed: 320 kilometer per hour or 200 miles per hour.
  (http://en.wikipedia.org/wiki/List_of_birds_by_flight_speed)

Why all this? It is to show us that there is nothing that can stop the eagles from arriving at their destinations. Do you know that there is traffic in the air? I learned about this during my domestic and international flights. Sometimes, the pilots would announce that due to some traffic in the air, the aircraft would not be able to take off or land. Traffic in the air? I soliloquized. But yes. There is traffic in the air and they are real. From this, I learned that there is traffic in life. There is seen and unseen traffic. There is physical and spiritual traffic. There is natural and supernatural traffic. There is emotional and psychological traffic. There is economic and financial traffic. There is marital and relational traffic. There is traffic that will delay your takeoff and landing. There is traffic that will delay and deny you from reaching your destination. There is much traffic. What is your own traffic?

But here is the truth: eagles are not hindered by air traffic. When other birds fly low, they fly higher. When other birds fly slowly, they fly the fastest. When other birds are contemplating and complaining, they fly with high speed. When other birds are procrastinating, they proceed. When other birds settle for complacence, they reach for excellence. When other birds are wishing, they are willing. When other birds are playing, they are flying. They do not allow the traffic in the air to stop them for soaring. They maintain their lanes in the traffic. They do not compete with other birds in the traffic. They do not yell or curse. Instead, they maintain their speed.

Many people have allowed the traffic of life to slow them down. They have given up trying to fly because they are afraid and have many excuses. They complain about many things in their lives that have slowed them down. They have allowed their complaints, negative and critical attitudes to turn them to chickens. They only see problems and why they cannot and can never do it. They never see any positive side of life. Life to them is full of problems. They have allowed circumstances and traffic in life to slow them down. Many have become parked cars and it has been said that, *"It is dangerous to follow a parked car."*

Maybe I need to ask you these questions: What is your present speed level? Are you speeding at your capacity? Have you allowed the traffics of life to slow you down or to make you quit? Always remember that eagles will always run the fastest and not crawl like chickens. What are you doing? Are you running or still crawling? God can enable you to overtake those who have gone ahead of you only if you can realize the power of that is in you. Hear what the Lord does as revealed in Isaiah 40:29, *"He gives power to the faint and weary, and to him who has no might He increases strength [causing it to multiply and making it to abound]."* (Amplified) May be you need to stop and ask for His power and strength that will increase your speeding level in life.

Walking

"They shall walk and not faint..." (NKJV)

Eagles do not only run and speed, but also walk slowly. The slow moment is when eagles try to catch up with one another. They cannot afford to leave others behind. The mother eagles must take it slow with the baby eagles so that they can maintain leverage. It is not how fast you get there, but how patient you are to get there. That eagles maintain a speed does not mean that they must not be considerate of others. They do not run others down to get there. They are not selfish in their desire to soar and speed. They believe that success is not being there alone, but bringing others along with you. How many people have you carried along with you? Yes, you have reached there, but how many people have you helped up?

Hear what Deuteronomy 32:11 says: *"The LORD was like an eagle teaching its young to fly, always ready to **swoop down** and catch them on its back."* (Contemporary English Version) The Lord, our Creator and Maker, stooped down by becoming like man in order to help us get to where He has destined for us. The Lord became man in Jesus Christ. He walked on this Earth for 33 years to give us power and strength to walk toward our destinies. He identified with us. He held us in His hands. He was with us in our boats of life. He gave us meaning and purpose for our lives. No wonder the writer of the Book of Hebrews has this to say about Him: *"For we do not have a High Priest Who is unable to understand and sympathize and have a shared feeling with our weaknesses and infirmities and liability to the assaults of temptation, but One Who has been tempted in every respect as we are, yet without sinning."* (Hebrews 4:15, Amplified) Because of this we are given these words of encouragement in the following verse" *"Let us then fearlessly and confidently and boldly draw near to the throne of grace (the throne of God's unmerited favor to us sinners), that we may receive mercy [for our failures] and find grace to help in good time for every need [appropriate help and well-timed help, coming just when we need it]."* (Hebrews 4:16, Amplified) Jesus stooped and slowed down so that we can stand up. Without Him becoming the Son of Man we cannot become Sons of God.

How many people have you stooped down for? How many people are you caring for and carrying along? Are you flying alone or are you flying with others? Moses, the great man of God, carried Joshua along. Elijah, the fire brand prophet of God, carried Elisha with him. Jesus Christ, our Lord and Savior, carried the twelve apostles along. Barnabas, who was also known as the son of encouragement, carried Paul and John Mark along. Paul, the greatest apostle, carried people like Apollos, Timothy, Gaius, and Phoebe along with him. How many people have you enabled, motivated, inspired, cared for, and carried along with you to help to better their lives just as you have bettered your life? Many people want to be there alone. They want people to worship them. They want to become heroes instead of role models.

Life is not only about speeding; it is also about walking. You have to begin your walk by walking with God. Walking in life is both vertical and horizontal. You have to walk with God and you have to walk with people. However, your walk with God would determine your walk with people. The baby eagles learn to walk with mother eagles first before they begin to fly. The same way, you must learn to walk with God first, before you can reach any height in life. No wonder the Bible says this about Enoch, the first man that walked with God in the Bible, *"Enoch walked steadily with God. And then one day he was simply gone: God took him"* (Genesis 5:24, The Message Bible)

Seeing

Even this is not found in our Bible text, but I want to add this point as it shows one of the characteristics of eagles. Eagles see the farthest. It has been verified and attested that eagles have extremely keen eyesight, which enables them to spot potential prey from a very long distance. In other words, they can see farther and the farthest than other birds. This is called vision. It is the ability to see beyond the now and beyond the present. When other birds are searching, eagles are seeing because they operate by vision and not by emotion.

Ornithology or the research or study of birds has revealed eagles have two foveae or centers of focus, that allow the birds to see both forward and to the side at the same time. They are capable of seeing fish in the water from several hundred feet above, while soaring, gliding or in flapping flight. Eagles' eyes are almost as large as those of humans, but they are sharper four times more than those of humans. They have perfect visions. Eagles are able to spot a rabbit moving almost a mile away. This shows that an eagle that is flying at about altitude of 1000 feet over open country is able to see and detect any prey over an area of almost 3 square miles from a fixed position. (http://www.baldeagleinfo.com/eagle/eagle2.html) What great vision!

Life is like a mission. But it takes vision to fulfill or accomplish the mission of life. No wonder the Bible says, *"Where there is no vision, the people perish."* (Proverbs 29:18, KJV) Vision is what defines who you are and what you will become in life. You have to see it, perceive it, and believe it. Isaiah began his ministry in Isaiah chapter 6 by seeing the vision of God, the vision of himself, and the vision of the world. Apostle Paul began his apostolic ministry after he had seen the vision of the risen Christ and the Church confirmed the vision by heeding to the command of the Holy Spirit in Acts 13:1-2. Moses saw the vision of God and his mission through the unconsumed burning bush.

Without vision you cannot have conviction. Without vision you cannot have motivation. Without vision you cannot have passion. Without vision you cannot have inspiration. Without vision you cannot have direction. Vision gives you foresight instead of eyesight. Vision gives you direction instead of distraction. Vision keeps you going. Vision keeps you focused. Vision makes you see beyond the past, the present, and the circumstances.

The eagles can see farther beyond the present. In the same way, you must be able to see beyond now and from the known to the unknown. What is the level of your vision? Do you pursue your vision? Do you have a vision? Do you know where you are going? Like eagles, God has given you the power to see beyond your present to where He is taking you to. Don't let where you are blind you to see where you are going. But you have to see by faith and not by sight. Always remember this: *How far you see will determine how far you will go in life. Your vision is the key to your mission.*

There is the power of eagles in everyone. It is must be discovered, recovered, and uncovered. You are more than what you think you are. The Lord says: you are an eagle. You have the power to wait on the Lord; you have the power to renew your strength; you have the power to fly higher; you have the power to move faster; you have the power to see farther; and you have the power to influence others positively.

As you finish reading this book, may the Lord help you and give you strength to activate and operate with the power of eagles that is in you. Amen. May the Lord help you to see the potentials, greatness, and excellence that is in you. Therefore, you need to redefine yourself and your life in the light of what God says that you are and not in what the system says that you are. Excellence in life can be earned, achieved, accomplished, and realized. But the real excellence is earned through Jesus Christ. No wonder Paul said, Christ in you the hope of glory. It is His glory in you that produces your glory. It is His excellence in you that produces your excellence in life.

CPSIA information can be obtained at www.ICGtesting.com
Printed in the USA
BVOW08s1159290915

420159BV00002B/3/P